KIDS IN CASKETS

the stunning dereliction of America's grown-ups

CAROL BENGLE GILBERT

979-8-9881056-1-9

Cover design by Stefanie Fontecha, Beetiful Book Covers..

This book is dedicated to the extinguished dreams of the children we allow to die from gunshots.

ABOUT THIS BOOK

You'll find a realistic fiction story filling the left-hand (even-numbered) pages. Written in the style of a children's easy reader, the story destroys any sliver of illusion that American adults protect our children from bullets blasting open their heads.

As you read the right-hand pages, try not to sob as the shameful and heartless truth of how we let child after child die pummels you. You'll meet each and every American baby, preschooler, grade schooler, and teenager whose body was ripped apart by bullets in just the first month of 2023. See how thick this book is? Feeling a bit squeamish?

50% of the net profits from the sales of this book are donated to individuals suffering the effects of a child's gun death or organizations providing direct aid to families shattered by a child gun death or working to prevent such deaths.

Note to readers: the subject of the nonfiction story in this book is child gun deaths. It draws from public reporting concerning real children who died. It contains, on page 70, a photograph sourced from a medical journal showing what a single gunshot wound to the face looks like.

January 2023

One ordinary month in the lives of
America's children

"Who will protect the children?"

"Not me," said Jeremy Gunslinger. "They can fend for themselves."

Just then, a gunshot rang out, and another child fell to the ground, lifeless.

"Oh, dear," said Wanda Wishywashy. "I wish there was something we could do."

January 1, 2023

January 1st was not "Happy New Year" for eight American families. For them, the year started with a BANG!, their children dead of gunshots.

LYRIC THOMAS
Age 5
Charlotte, N.C.

The New Year had barely started when life ended for 5-year-old Lyric Thomas, the little girl her daddy described as a ball of joy. Inside a Charlotte, North Carolina residence, a family member found Lyric dead from a gunshot. The police called it "an accident" and declined to release details. An accident? A gun is a deadly weapon. A little girl doesn't die of a gunshot in the absence of adult negligence or wrongdoing. Lyric didn't get to see what 2023 would bring. Nor will she dance at her prom, build a career, or share a golden anniversary. Lyric is avoidably dead at 5 years of age.

AMETHYST SISTINE SILVA
Age 11
Corpus Christi, TX

Parents are eager to hear their babies' first words. Not their last. Amethyst's last word was "ouch." That's what she said when the gunshot hit her. It wasn't supposed to happen this way. Amethyst was outside her apartment building with her parents watching the celebratory fireworks to ring in the New Year. Her parents took some photos beforehand to mark the happy occasion. They didn't expect the horrifying turn of events any more than they expected those photos to be the last ones they'd

The news came on. An ideological extremist (some people called him a "crackpot," for short) shot up an elementary school. Many children died. It was the third school shooting in as many months.

ones they'd ever take of their lively daughter. A couple of men with guns fired wildly to "celebrate." One of their bullets pierced Amethyst's back. She was pronounced dead at 11 years old.

ADELE JONES
Age 15
Chicago, IL

Adele was driving a stolen car with three other male teenagers inside when a car pulled up alongside them and one of its occupants fired a gun repeatedly. The other teens were injured. Adele died.

JARVIS WATTS
Age 9
Chicago, IL

Jarvis used to help one of his neighbors carry her groceries inside. When he had to take his family's trash to the curb, he would take hers, too, if she happened to need it. Another neighbor recounted how Jarvis played basketball with her son who has special needs.

At an extended-family gathering, Jarvis was one of 6 children between ages 2 and 10 told to go upstairs and get ready for bed. A mystery gun whose existence the adults in the house disavowed any knowledge of, and which vanished before police arrived, was fired by someone. The other children said Jarvis played with the gun and shot himself unintentionally. He had been shot multiple times. The coroner ruled the shooting a homicide. None of that matters to Jarvis; he stumbled down the stairs calling for his mother, then collapsed, face down on the living room floor. His life was over at age 9.

"Thoughts and prayers," posted the mayor online.

"We'll serve up justice to the man who did it," said the chief of police.

"*Somebody* needs to do *something*," shrilled the newspaper editor. "This needs to stop."

D'ASIA GARRISON
Age 16
Baltimore, MD
D'Asia was shot to death outside an East Baltimore home where police found cars and buildings pocked with bullet holes in the early hours of the New Year. The murder resulted from an unspecified dispute.

STEVEN PERKINS
Age 17
Milwaukee, WI
Steven was in a fast food restaurant when another young man with a gun shot him.

JOSEPH IVORY, JR.
Age 16
Grand Rapids, MI
Joseph, nicknamed JoJo, was a gang member who was taking baby steps toward turning his life around after becoming a father 10 months earlier. He and friends from the gang had been shooting off guns to celebrate the New Year. He was driving away from the celebratory shooting scene in a stolen car when he was shot.

KESHAWN NEVERE BANKS
Age 16
Saginaw, MI
Keshawn was with others in a car at a gas station when someone shot at them, killing him and injuring an adult woman.

The teacher told the kids to huddle in a corner silently. "Pretend men with automatic rifles are hunting you," she told them.

THE FIRST DAY OF THE YEAR 2023 ENDS: 8 AMERICAN KIDS AGES 5 TO 17 BATTERED TO DEATH BY BULLETS, COMMITTED TO THE BONEYARD FOR ETERNITY.

Image by brgfx on Freepik

JANUARY 2, 2023

Another day dawns, another child dies from gun blasts. And then another. And another. And another. And another. Wait, there's one more.

GIRL, NAME NOT RELEASED
Age 6
Spring, Texas

The house was still decorated from her 6th and last birthday party when the little girl's teenage siblings found her and her mother dead in their Spring, Texas home. This little girl was murdered with a gun in her own home by her own mother. Her identity wasn't released. Her right to live, indeed her entire future, was snuffed out by a bullet. And no one even knows what her name was.

NAYSHAWN LOVETT
Age 16
Mansfield, OH

A man shot Nayshawn multiple times in the stairwell of a motel, killing him.

The principal said on the loudspeaker, "If a real shooter comes in, pretend you're already dead. He might pass you by."

"Oh, and if the kid next to you is bleeding out," the principal added, "wipe some of their blood on your face so your pretend death looks more convincing."

MARTEZ TONEY
Age 17
Washington, D.C.

Mild-mannered, 17-year-old Martez Toney was reported to be the first child gun homicide victim in DC in 2023. It's reported as a first for the year because the media knows there will be more kids shot dead with each passing day. This particular high school student died while standing at the bus bay at the Congress Heights Metro station. Police found a ghost gun nearby.

JAMIL THORNTON
Age 17
Detroit, MI

Jamil was arguing with his 26-year-old brother when his 29-year-old cousin pulled out a gun and shot both of them. Jamil died at the scene, and his brother died later at the hospital. The cousin fled the home and later killed himself.

JAMES MARTIN
Age 15
Indianapolis, IN

James died in his home due to an unintentional shooting by another person. The details were hushed up so we can't truly understand what happened or what we might do to prevent something like it from happening again.

JEREMIAH ROBERGEAU
Age 15
Ft. Lauderdale, FL

Jeremiah's favorite color was red, so that's the color his friends and family wore to the posthumous candlelight vigil for the boy they called "JC." He was shot while walking down the street.

The children's faces were somber.

Then there was another shooting and more children dead. This time it happened in their town.

JANUARY 3, 2023

MICHAEL MASON
Age 16
Indianapolis, IN

Michael and a friend were leaving a shopping mall and walked up to what they mistakenly believed was Michael's car— it was the same color, make, and model. As Michael reached for the door handle, the boys realized their mistake. But a man in the backseat was already starting to shoot. Six bullets struck Michael and killed him. The other boy attempted to run but fell and the shooter pursued him and shot him. The shooter said he was afraid the boys intended to rob him. He was arrested on multiple charges including voluntary manslaughter.

TEENAGER
Age between 11-17
Monticello, AK

One teenager was shot to death and another suffered gunshot wounds in what police described as a "disturbance" at a residence.

EVONNA JACKSON
Age 14
New Orleans, LA

Evonna, her father, and her uncle were victims of a triple homicide in their longtime home. Bullet casings were found on the floor by their bodies. They had been dead several days by the time their bodies were discovered.

SCARLETT TUCKER
Age 16
Burlington, KY

Scarlett spent the evening out and about with friends, a 17-year-old female, 18-year-old female, and an 18-year-old male. They then returned to the home of the 18-year-old female friend. When a bag of marijuana fell onto the bedroom floor, the male demanded that Scarlett pick it up. She refused, and he shot her dead.

The children balked when their parents tried to load them onto the school buses. They cried and shook. Some became moody and quiet. They got tummy aches. They protested, "I'm too tired" when asked to help around the house or do their homework and even when Dad said, "Let's go out for ice cream."

JANUARY 4, 2023

JOURNEE CARROLL WARD
Age 3
Dumfries, VA

Journee Carroll Ward loved to dance and sing. She was often the life of the party. But three months after 3-year-old Journee and her siblings arrived in Dumfries to live with their grandmother after their mother's sudden death, Journee herself was dead. One of Journee's teenage sisters and her boyfriend had an argument that day over a food subsidy card. The boyfriend shot and gravely wounded several members of the family. Journee, the baby girl who wiped away her siblings' tears when they cried over their mother's death, was now dead herself.

LIAM BRUECHE
Age 5
Florissant, CO

Like so many little boys his age, Liam's eyes lit up when he encountered cars, trucks, and dirt. He traveled by bike and scooter. Liam's father was a convicted felon who by law couldn't buy a handgun or assault weapon; instead, since the state's red flag law excludes air rifles, he used a compressed air rifle to murder Liam before committing suicide, avoiding a court-ordered exchange of custody. No more playing in the dirt or whizzing around on his bike for Liam. His life is over, at age 5.

DEANTA DORSEY
Age 16
Baltimore, MD

Deanta was outside a Popeye's Restaurant at a shopping mall in Baltimore with fellow high school students on lunch break from school when two young men shot at the group, assassinating Deanta with 18 bullets. The four other high school students with him were also shot but survived. A 16-year-old was later charged with first-degree murder in Deanta's death.

And still the adults did nothing.

Well, they did "tut-tut" when the next shooting happened.

And the people elected to represent them in our government once again issued press releases. They wanted everyone to know that their "thoughts and prayers" were with this new round of dead children and their families.

BRANDON BANKS
Age 17
Indianapolis, IN

At 17, Brandon Banks was found dead of a gunshot inside a vehicle. Should we ask why?

BRAYDEN WRANA
Age 14
Mineral City, OH

Brayden was a friendly boy who played baseball. One evening when his parents were out and he was in the house with his little sister and brother, he decided to play with the handgun his parents kept in his home "for protection." He unintentionally shot himself in the head. It was his 11-year-old sister who had to call 911 and then perform CPR in a futile effort to resuscitate him. Their 9-year-old brother was there to watch his sister's desperate attempts to bring their big brother back to life. Their parents were at the hospital visiting other relatives who'd been injured in a crash earlier in the day when they got the news.

SH'MAYA ANDERSON
Age 15
Jackson, MS

Sh'Maya was known for being friendly and athletic. She was walking to a store with friends one day when another kid emerged from a car and shot her a total of 8 times. Her family knew instantly who was responsible for shooting her, indicating there had been an earlier dispute between two groups of kids.

Congress whispered about gun control.

"Let's ban the assault rifles," said the bravest among them. "No one needs a gun that can shoot 300 rounds per minute."

BRECK GERARD WILLIAMS, JR.
Age 17
Fort Worth, TX

ADRIAN DANIELS
Age 14
Fort Worth, TX

Breck was looking forward to getting an apartment of his own and trying to get a foothold in the music industry. Adrian was an honor roll student and an athlete. Both were shot outside the home of another teen. That teen was also shot but survived.

There hasn't been a single child dead of a gunshot in a school massacre or large venue shooting up to this point. Yet the gun deaths are mounting. 10 of the 26 American children (38%) dead from gun violence in only the first four days of 2023— yes, we're only 4 days in— died inside their own homes or homes of family/friends. <u>When there's a gun in the house, children are not safe.</u> Isn't those children's fundamental right to remain alive, to have an opportunity to grow up, more Constitutionally-sacred than an adult's right to keep a gun in the house?

"We have the right to own any guns we want," snarled the objectors.

"We *need* guns to protect our families."

"No one has the right to tell us what we can and can't do."

JANUARY 5, 2023

MACIE HAIGHT
Age 17
Enoch, UT

BRILEY HAIGHT
Age 12
Enoch, UT

AMMON HAIGHT
Age 7
Enoch, UT

SIENNA HAIGHT
Age 7
Enoch, UT

GAVIN HAIGHT
Age 4
Enoch, UT

They were brothers and sisters. Four-year-old Gavin, the youngest, loved superheros and drawing on the wall (even though Mommy told him not to.) The twins, 7-year-old Sienna and Ammon shared a love of riddles and jokes but nurtured independent interests as well. Sienna adored cats; Ammon liked to play with Legos. Briley displayed musical talent on both piano and cello. At 12, she'd given thought to her future already. The voracious reader planned to become a librarian. The oldest sibling Macie had dreams, too. She looked forward to going to college in the fall and to one day becoming a mother.

Macie had done her utmost to protect herself and her siblings, alerting Child Protective Services and police that since 2017 her father had been assaulting her and other family members; in her case, it was choking,

"Good guys with guns will save us from the bad guys with guns," shouted the folks who refuse to hear any evidence that contradicts their opinions. (They suffer from a stubbornly persevering aversion to facts.)

"We'll put armed police in every school. Metal detectors, too."

banging her head on furniture, and shaking her in anger. All of the children had red marks on their necks from the car seatbelts chafing them the day she reported that her father had swerved the car furiously to scare them. And her mother had confirmed the report of Macie's father throwing Ammon, then 5, to the ground when he protested going to school.

Macie, the protective older sister will never go to college or become a mommy herself. Briley will never share her love of books with library patrons. No more cats for Sienna or Legos for Ammon. Neither of whom will ever again giggle at a silly riddle. Gavin's crayons have been put away forever. With divorce pending, their father shot all five of them dead, as they slept, along with their mother and maternal grandmother. With a gun kept for protecting the family.

CRAIG CURTIS, JR.
Age 16
Raleigh, NC
A teenage friend unintentionally shot Craig Curtis to death with an AR-15 in his own home shortly after his 16th birthday. The friend brought the assault weapon into Craig's home.

CARNELIUS WILLIAMS
Age 17
Little Rock, AR
Carnelius was shot in the road. Who knows why! It seems we aren't in the habit of demanding answers when children are shot dead.

TERRIEK JAMES
Age 15
New Orleans, LA
Terriek was shot on Canal St. and dropped off at a hospital where he later died.

"What about the mall shootings?"

"Armed security in every mall!"

"And the stadiums? The parade routes? The concert halls?"

"More guns will fix this."

They chanted, "More guns. More guns. More guns."

JANUARY 6, 2023

KAYLA LYNN WALKER
Age 16
Detroit, MI
A group of siblings were playing Uno in their living room. Someone outside shot a gun through the window hitting Kayla and killing her.

TEEN
Age 17
North Little Rock, AR
Died of a gunshot wound inflicted inside a home. Who was this child? Who shot him? Why?

TEEN
Age 17
Chicago, IL
The teenager stopped at a gas station when someone came up and shot him and the teen with him multiple times. He died from his injuries. And, again, no name reported.

> Demand to know their names and their stories! Remembering them is the least we can do. They died because we didn't work hard enough to protect them.

BRYAN SANCHEZ
Age 15
Odessa, TX
Bryan was shot dead in a robbery. Another teenager confessed to the killing.

One man's eyes lit up. "I know just what to do," he exclaimed. "We'll force 'em to buy see-through backpacks (at a premium price). And we'll tell the parents their kids need oh-so-expensive bullet-proof clothing."

He rubbed his hands together in anticipation and licked his lips.

JANUARY 7, 2023

MACKENZIE HAGGER
Age 10
Fennville, MI

AUTUMN HAGGER
Age 13
Fennville, MI

Autumn loved horses and softball. She looked forward to her upcoming 14th birthday and learning to drive. She was pondering a future in dermatology. Autumn's little sister Mackenzie was in fourth grade, a girly girl who loved sunflowers and makeup. It was their father who turned a shotgun on them and murdered them inside their own home, along with their mother. Their mother had expressed an intention to end the marriage due to abuse.

KARON BLAKE
Age 13
Washington, D.C.

Karon Blake was a fashion-loving sixth grader who enjoyed football. His school described him as a quiet and inquisitive scholar. Karon and some friends made a very bad decision. They went for a ride in a stolen car late one night and ended up walking along a neighborhood street, looking into cars with a flashlight. A local resident believed they were tampering with the cars and came out with a gun, shooting at Karon who repeatedly shouted "I am sorry," "Please, don't," "No," and "I'm a kid" as the bullets flew until the fatal shot felled him.

NYLA CRAYTON
Age 16
Highpoint, NC

NASIR CRAYTON
Age 10
Highpoint, NC

Another man puts his gun to his children's heads and pulls the trigger. Nyla Crayton, 16, dead. Nasir Crayton,

While the reasonable members of Congress whispered and the rest made noise, word came that a father, distraught over an impending divorce, shot all five of his children dead— with the gun he kept "to protect his family."

10, dead. Also dead, an 18 year old son and the children's mother. Not dead, but devastated: the young adult son who woke up to find his father putting a gun to his head and grabbed the gun, pulling out the magazine. He and a female visitor who escaped the terror with him ran to a neighbor for help, but it was too late. There were warnings, a history of police calls and an involuntary mental health order served a year earlier. But the unstable man had a "right" to own guns, and two innocent children are dead of gun violence as a result.

> Who's mentally sick?
> The shooters or us, the people standing by while one American child after another falls down dead to gunshots?

GIANCARLOS RIVERA-LOPEZ
Age 17
Columbus, GA
Giancarlos was shot outside an apartment complex and died at the scene. The teen had wanted to become a music artist.

TREONTE 'TRE' JOHNSON
Age 17
Iberia, LA
Trea adored his baby sister. He also liked to dance, rap, and play ball. He was home alone with the baby the night he got a call to come outside. He stepped outside and was met with a hail of bullets.

KAI'BIENN BOOKHART
Age 16
Santee, SC
Kai'Bienn was shot to death by an 18-year-old acquaintance who turned himself in after the shooting.

That same day, a curious baby boy found the gun Mommy kept in her purse "to protect herself and her baby." He put it to his head, saying playfully, "Bang. Bang." Before Mommy could grab the gun, he pulled the trigger and Mommy watched in horror as his life was dribbling away.

ALEXANDER DELGADO
Age 16
Nashville, TN

Alexander was shot in the head while driving, causing his vehicle to crash into an IHOP. Alex had a year and a half left before he would have graduated from high school and looked forward to that milestone.

GAVIN D. "POOKIE" BEIGHLEY
Age 17
Sharon, PA

Pookie was a social kid who loved hanging out with friends and enjoyed camping and kayaking, as well as riding his bike. He was on his bicycle alongside three of his friends when a 19-year-old started shooting at them from 200-300 yards away without provocation. He died.

TEEN
Age 15
Oakland, CA

The boy was in a car with a friend when bullets from outside struck him. He died of his injuries.

HOW MANY DAYS? HOW MANY BULLETS?

THE FIRST WEEK OF 2023 ENDS WITH 49 KIDS DEAD FROM GUNSHOTS. KIDS WHO WILL REMAIN DEAD FOREVER AND WON'T BE COMING BACK. IT'S ON US. THE ADULTS. WE HAD THE POWER TO PROTECT THEM. WE DIDN'T USE IT.

JANUARY 8, 2023

JAMES LETT, JR.
Age 12
Tampa, Florida

A group of teenage boys were playing with a gun one of them brought into the house when a 14-year-old, thinking it was not loaded, pointed it at the back of

There was a calamitous crossfire of press conferences on the steps of the Capitol.

One side shouted, "More guns."

The other side screamed, "Ban assault rifles."

While the crowd strained to make out the speakers' words, another "crackpot" entered a grocery store.

ames' head and pulled the trigger. James was sitting on a bed playing video games on his phone, unaware of what was coming. He died when the bullet blasted through his head. A 15-year-old with him was injured after the bullet sped out of the front side of James' head and struck him in the mouth.

KHAIBIR HOLMES
Age 14
Goldsboro, NC

Khaibir was playing basketball at a local park when a fight broke out and someone shot him and an adult man multiple times.

MARQUARIUS CARPENTER
Age 17
Jackson, MS

Marquarius was found dead in the street, felled by multiple gunshot wounds. He was blocks from his home when he was shot. Two adults were arrested for the shooting. Marquarius was under house arrest and wearing an ankle monitor.

JUAN VIVEROS
Age 15
Dinuba, CA

Juan was shot to death and two other minors with him were shot but survived.

JACQUELINE NUNEZ-MILLAN
Age 16
Circleville, UT

Jackie was the wrestling team's stat girl, played various sports and was also a cheerleader at her high school. Her 17-year-old boyfriend shot her to death.

TEEN
Age 17
Houston, TX

Shots were fired into the car in which this boy was riding with friends. His friends mistakenly drove him to an

Wiped out in a deadly instant:

- a great-grandmother and her great-grandson,
- a cooing infant in her big brother's arms,
- a tired dad and his toddler stopping for diapers on their way home from work and daycare, and
- two giggling preteen girls.

assisted living facility instead of a hospital as he was dying.

AMIR MOORE
Age 16
Kansas City, MO
Amir was a joyful boy whose smile lit up the room. Someone fired shots into a car in which he was riding, killing him and extinguishing his beautiful smile.
.

JANUARY 9, 2023

AVERI JONES
Age 1
Jonestown, MS

BOY, NAME NOT RELEASED
Age 9
Jonestown, MS
An acquaintance of Averi's mother who was staying with them put a pillow over the sleeping baby's head and shot her dead. He used the same gun to murder the 9-year-old boy whose name was not released. No one knows why he did it, but until we decide we're going to do something about all of these children dying from gunshots, how much does the "why" matter?

DARRIS ANDERSON, JR.
Age 17
Ferguson, MO
Darris was sitting in a car when someone fired a gun and killed him.

TRENTON KNIGHT
Age 17
Oklahoma City, OK
Several teenagers were in a home posting videos of themselves with guns online when one of them pulled the trigger, killing Trenton. The shooter claimed the

"Why isn't anyone doing anything to stop this?" asked the people angrily. "Why does this keep happening?"

They held a vigil with candles and signs saying, "No more gun violence" and "Save our children."

death resulted from gun "play;" Trenton's mother believed it was intentional.

ASHTON ROBERTS
Age 15
Macon, GA

Ashton Roberts was shot and killed by a man shooting from inside a marijuana grow house The killer fired fifteen rounds with several hitting Ashton, ultimately killing him. He almost made it home, falling against his front door, bleeding out.

ANGELINA HARRISON
Age 17
Cheyenne, WY

Angelina loved doing her make-up, hanging out with friends and going to car meets. She was thinking about becoming an attorney or a cosmetologist. But the 17-year-old will have neither of those careers; she was

shot to death. She was riding in the passenger seat of a car with another girl driving and two boys in the backseat. The boys were handling a gun and one of them activated the trigger, unintentionally shooting her.

TEEN
Age 17
Hopewell, VA

A boy whose name we don't know, whose story we won't hear is no longer. He was shot to death at Wales Mobile Home Park.

TEEN
Age 13
Pineland, TX

A 13-year-old girl committed suicide, using a gun, in her home.

By the time the vigil was over, another child was shot dead.

This boy knocked on a door to ask for directions. The man inside didn't like his looks, so he ended the boy's life with a smug smirk. And his gun of course. One of the thirteen he kept to protect his home from "people like that."

TEEN
Age 16
Wildomar, CA
Police believe that a conflict between the boy who was killed and one or more other minors led to this fatal shooting.

JANUARY 10, 2023

SHANE HAMILTON
Age 16
Baytown, TX
Shane had just celebrated his 16th birthday. The high school star athlete was returning from a basketball game when other students apparently followed him home and shot him on his doorstep.

AKIR MUHAMMED
Age 17
Decatur, GA
Akir had a job working as a valet parker while studying to become an electrician. Akir was the victim of an attempted robbery as he walked out of a gas station.

JANUARY 11, 2023

NOAH RODRIGUEZ
Age 15
Lubbock, TX
Noah and other minors were handling a gun. One of them must have activated the trigger because "it discharged," killing Noah.

SEMAJ RICHARDSON
Age 16
Philadelphia, PA
Semaj was found shot to death in a vacant lot near his home. Three teens, two of whom were seen shooting in a surveillance video, were believed to be responsible for his death.

When a Senator's despairing teenage daughter shot herself to death in the family's garage, it was her father's gun she used. She knew the combination to his gun safe because she'd seen him lock and unlock it many times.

AALIYAH CORTEZ
Age 16
Denver, CO

Aliyah was in a car being driven by her older sister. The girls were on their way to see their grandmother. On the way, the sister planned to sell some vape pens to someone she connected with online. Confused about the directions, she stopped the car at a stop sign to consult the GPS. The 17-year-old "buyer" came up to the car and put a gun to her head; she threw the vape cartridges out the window and tried to drive off as he held onto the car frame. Aliyah jumped across the seat pushing him, trying to dislodge him from the car frame. He shot Aliyah. The girls didn't have their visit with grandma that day. Instead, what was left of Aliyah, her dead body, went to the mortuary.

JANUARY 12, 2023

XAVIAR SIESS
Age 14
Tacoma, Washington

Xaviar was killed in a drive-by shooting while standing at by bus stop with three other teens. He's remembered by those who knew him as bright and generous .

A'RHIANNA MOYE
Age 13
Louisville, GA

A'rhianna's 17-year-old brother shot her in the neck inside her grandparents' home. For two weeks, her classmates wore pink to support her recovery from her wounds. Sadly, A'Rhianna didn't recover. The girl who was cheer captain and came in second in the Miss Seventh Grade competition won't be attending 8th grade. Police were uncertain whether the shooting was intentional.

When a distraught mother being punched by her husband ran and grabbed the gun they kept on a high shelf, warning him to stay back, he overpowered her and shot her dead, then used the gun to murder their two little girls.

JANUARY 13, 2023

JADYN BAEZ
Age 16
Cleveland, OH

Jadyn was a martial arts aficionado. He was shot in the head by his uncle who moved from room to room in Jayden's house, executing family members and friends of the family. Jadyn's mother and grandfather also died, along with a family friend. That friend's elementary-school-aged daughter was shot but survived.

RAJON LATEEF JACKSON III
Age 17
Waldorf, MD

An 18-year-old man, known to Rajon, shot at him from a car as he walked home from school, and several bullets struck him. Rajon died of his injuries.

DWAYNE SCOTT DZUBAY-PERCY
Age 15
Minneapolis, MN

Dwayne's nickname was Dweezy. He was on the "A" honor roll at Patrick Henry High School, won sports trophies, and was a former grass dancer and current member of the Mille Lacs band of Ojibwe. He was sitting in a stolen car with other teens inside when the driver of a van that had been at the same gas station as the teens earlier pursued them and shot into the car, killing Dwayne.

JANUARY 14, 2023

BRYAN PEREZ
Age 15
Phoenix, AZ

When two boys took food items from a gas station convenience store without paying and got into a car, the clerk chased them down, firing at them before and after they got in the car. Bryan was a passenger who never left

"Couldn't have predicted it," said some of the deniers.

"Mental illness," others droned.

the car, not one of the boys who stole from the store. He was killed by the gunshots.

EVAN WESSLING
Age 14
Tow, TX

Evan was a freshman at Burnet High School. He and his father were said to be very much alike. Silly. Fun. Two 19-year-olds shot them as they stood in their driveway. No motive for the shootings has been uncovered.

RYAN DONNELL MARABLE
Age 17
Birmingham, AL

Ryan's dead body was found in a backyard surrounded by shell casings. What if this happened to your son? Ryan was somebody's son.

JANUARY 15, 2023

DE'EVAN MCFALL
Age 11
Dallas, TX

De'Evan had talent. Basketball. Football. He also had a bright smile. He lost his life and the world lost that smile when his teenage sister and another girl, 14, got into a fight outside the apartment building where they lived; the other girl shot at De'Evan's sister but hit De'Evan instead.

American adults gone AWOL:
Who's protecting our children?

As the dead body count of America's children soared, remiss bystanders gathered up dollar bills and 5-spots for the survivors. They shook their heads, sadly, waiting for that indescribable *someone* to do that indefinable *something*.

JUSTYCE BROADWAY-WILLIAMS
Age 16
Des Plaines, IL

Justyce was thinking ahead to what he might want to do with his life. He was considering careers as an engineer or maybe a police officer. But Justyce won't have a career. He was found dead in the road on a quiet residential street. Neighbors reported hearing the gunshots that killed him, but no witnesses have come forward. He suffered several gunshot wounds.

WYATT OWENS
Age 16
Tacoma, WA

Wyatt was shot by someone in a passing car while driving. Police speculate the two drivers may have been racing or that the shooting may have been an act of road rage. Either way, Wyatt's dead, and America's moving on.

JAVARIOUS HENDRIX
Age 14
Louisville, KY

It was one of Javarious' friends who shot him dead, and Javarious' mother didn't know if the shooting was intentional or not. The boy who shot him was 11 or 12 years old and was with Javarious' brother in the brother's bedroom at the time of the shooting.

ENEDY PENEZOLA MORALES
Age 12
Winston-Salem, NC

Kids and adults gathered in a park watching a brawl take place. Enedy was one of them, in the park with her older sister.. Shots rang out— police believe more than one person was shooting— and Enedy was hit as she tried to run away but mistakenly ran into the path of a shooter. She later died from her injuries.

Although they were the adults, they didn't see it as their job to fix this. It was too big of a problem!

So they waited for someone they couldn't identify to do something (they weren't sure what) to stop the shooting scourge even as one American child after another was carried off to the graveyard.

TEEN
Age 17
Rockford, IL

Five people were shot inside an apartment, four adults and a minor. Three of them, including the minor, who was from Dallas, Texas, died of their injuries.

JANUARY 16, 2023

BREXIALEE TORRES-ORTIZ
Age 11
Syracuse, NY

Brexialee wanted peace and love, not just for herself but for everyone. Instead, she got two bullets in her midsection and a funeral. Sent to the store for a gallon of milk, Brexialee never came home. Three men drove by in a car, their gunshots apparently intended for a 19-year-old man nearby who was also shot but survived. Brexialee's hopes to play volleyball next year, gone. The sixth grader who loved to dance and play tennis, who served as student council president and excelled in math is in a grave. Forever. She was only 11.

BABY BOY, NAME NOT RELEASED
Age 2
Camden, AL

Shot, died, forgotten. His name never released. No news follow-up. No vigils. No public memorials. The baby was in a car with his mother when someone fired a bullet in his direction, and he took his last breaths.

VENUS RODRIGUEZ
Age 16
Oak Cliff, TX

Venus played the trumpet and once dreamed of becoming a beautician. But by the time she died, 16-year-old Venus was living with an abusive 22-year-old boyfriend she'd run away to be with four months earlier, days before her 16th birthday. He shot her to death in their apartment, then dumped her body in a creek.

When it was time for the highest court in the land to settle the squabble over what could and couldn't be done to stop more children from dying, the court looked to the past for a solution.

"What kind of gun control did they have in the 1600s?" the chief justice asked.

CHASE JONES
Age 13
Clairton, PA

Charming and goofy is how people used to describe Chase. Now, he's described as dead. Chase was playing video games with three other boys when one shot him. The shooter was 13. Chase died of his injuries. Before the shooting, Chase and the boy who shot him were best friends.

TEEN
Age 16
Gainesville, TX

This teen was killed along with a 19-year-old.

WILLIE CHARLES SMITH II
Age 16
Flint, MI

Willie was at a friend's house with other boys when someone pulled the trigger on a gun, shooting him to death. A 17-year-old was arrested and charged with negligent open murder and felony firearm use.

CORDARIAN HALL
Age 14
Nashville, TN

Cordarian and a 19-year-old man were both shot in North Nashville six miles from their homes. The older teen died at the scene. Cordarian was found in a ball field with shell casings around him. He died days later in the hospital.

JANUARY 17, 2023

TEEN
Age 12-17
Crowley, LA

Someone's child was shot and killed at the entrance to a subdivision. Police collected 30 high-powered rifle

"Why, none at all," said the justice two seats to his left.

casings from the scene. An adult victim was injured but survived.

JANUARY 18, 2023

ALISSA PARRAZ
Age 16
Goshen, CA

NYCHOLAS PARRAZ
10 months
Goshen, CA

A gang shooting took out an entire family in Goshen, California including a teenage mother who was chased down while gripping her 10-month-old baby boy. Alissa fled the home with her baby as the shooting began but the killers tracked her down and shot her and infant Nycholas outside. She had placed her baby over a fence in an effort to hide him but the shooters got him anyway. One adult member of the household was involved in a rival gang. The innocent children paid the price.

OSCAR BECK
Age 7
Fort Wayne, IN

Oscar was all into sports, Little League, basketball, football, wrestling. He liked to wear his favorite cap and pjs to school and play with the Magna Tiles. He lived in a nice neighborhood where everyone knew each other. But the safety was an illusion. There was a gun in Oscar's home and one day his mother used it to shoot him in the chest and then commit suicide.

"And you didn't see mass shootings with assault rifles," pronounced the justice on his immediate right, pleased with his own intellectual prowess.

JANUARY 19, 2023

JESSE LEPORE
Age 9
Murfreesboro, TN

SEAN LEPORE
Age 11
Murfreesboro, TN

The boys raced competitively. For Sean it was Quarter Midget and bandolero race cars, for Jesse BMX bikes. Now the boys who sped through life are still forever. On the run after bludgeoning the boys' mother several weeks earlier as a divorce loomed, their father shot them to death and then killed himself as the police closed in.

And each time the people said it was such a surprise.
They never would have expected it.
Such a nice family.

And you still think your family's different, don't you?
They did, too, until it happened in their family.

ADAUN GAINES
Age 5
Jennings, LA

Five children ages six and under were left unattended for a short time at home by their babysitter in a house with a stolen 9 mm handgun left loaded in a dresser drawer. As Adaun's 6-year-old cousin played with the gun, he unintentionally shot Adaun. The babysitter delayed getting medical attention for Adaun to give him time to hide the gun and a marijuana stash. He and the woman who was responsible for the gun being in the residence

"No one burst into colonial schoolhouses with high-capacity magazines, running from room to room, murdering children. Back then, you could wheel your shopping cart up and down the aisles of the grocery stores without a care in the world. And not once did we hear of a drive-by shooting committed by a colonist galloping down the interstate on horseback."

were arrested. The woman was mother to some of the children, including the one who pulled the trigger, and she was on probation for firearm violations, barred from gun ownership.

ADRIAN ESPARZA
Age 16
Wasco, CA

Adrian was shot in the head and died two days later.

TEEN
Age 16
Philadelphia, PA

Why was this teen boy shot twice in the chest and once in the stomach inside a house? The shooter, whoever it was, killed him. He also shot and injured two adult men.

MIYKA CRAWFORD
Age 14
Coolidge, Arizona

Mikya fell asleep in her living room while watching a movie. That was where she was killed. More than a dozen 9mm and 40 caliber bullets from a targeted drive-by shooting entered the home, and one penetrated Mikya's head. The children and adults arrested for the shooting ranged from age 14 to age 19. It may have been a guest in the home who was the target. Mikya wanted to become an entrepreneur, an opportunity stolen from her.

JANUARY 20, 2023

ZECHARIAH TREVINO
Age 17
Fort Worth, TX

His mother remembers how her jokester son once stole the meatballs she'd prepared for Thanksgiving dinner. She tenderly recalls how even at 6'3" her teenage son hadn't yet come to terms with thunderstorms or nightfall. He loved drawing, and a teacher had given him a sketching kit shortly before his death. He had a

The other justices grinned.

"That's the answer," they chortled in unison. "We do what the Americans who were not actually Americans because there was no America yet did back then."

part-time job at the Whataburger, and it's there that he died, shot outside his workplace. Zechariah protected his 16-year-old cousin who was with him when the bullets came, saving her life at the expense of his own. The shooters were other teens from his high school.

JOSUE LOPEZ-ORTEGA
Age 15
Bronx, NY

Josue and a friend had just left the Police Athletic League where they'd been playing basketball when a man jumped out of a car and shot into a crowd of people. Josue was killed and the other boy injured. The police believed the shooting was likely in response to an earlier dispute.

KRISTOPHER BACA
Age 17
Palmdale, CA

Kristopher Baca was walking to his grandmother's house when a car pulled up alongside where he was walking, an argument erupted between a car occupant and Kristopher, and the occupant fired several shots. Kristopher died from his injuries.

KWELIK BACOATE
Age 17
Darlington, SC

Two groups of young men got into a physical altercation that resulted in Kwelik being killed. The shooting was considered gang related.

JANUARY 21, 2023

DESHON DUBOSE
Age 13
Atlanta, GA

DeShon went ice skating, never to return home. The boy who was described as humble, an "old soul," and who thought he might become a pastor died as a bystander

And so the highest court in the land said that the answer to the problem of our children being shot dead in their homes, in the streets, in their schools, in places of worship, concert halls, and grocery stores was to do nothing.

Nothing at all.

to a fight that turned deadly, leaving. DeShon lying dead of a gunshot wound outside the skating rink.

ANTERRIUS 'LIL ANT' HILL
Age 12
Jefferson County, AL

Anterrius was found in his home just after midnight suffering from a gunshot wound. Police were questioning another boy thought to have been in the home about what happened.

SEBASTIAN FLORENTINO
Age 14
Milwaukee, WI

Sebastian and his 13-year-old brother were with other teens making videos in a vacant garage to show off guns. Another 14-year-old wielding a 9mm gun shot both of them. After shooting the first round into Sebastian, the 14-year-old shooter said "Sorry, bro" according to the criminal complaint and continued shooting. The 13-year-old survived by playing dead after he was shot.

KHALIL SALEEM
Age 17
Long Beach, CA

An exchange of gunfire between a stranger at the basketball courts and and teens in a car driving by took Khalil's life. He'd been looking forward to turning 18 in March so he could drive a car and go to prom.

LAMAR LESLIE ALLEN
Age 15
Windsor Mill, MD

Lamar was respectful, and his mother never thought she'd be the parent who'd get word her son was shot. The boy who hoped one day to run a trucking business is instead in his grave after being shot on the street.

TEEN
Age 13
Glenarden, Maryland

This boy used a shotgun to commit suicide.

As the justices announced the decision reflecting their collective wisdom (and the peculiar knotting of the law preferred by their most generous secret benefactors), word came that three more children had been shot in a drive-by, their bodies torn apart from the inside, and none of them survived.

CARLOS LUGO
Age 14
Houston, TX

Carlos was shot to death in a grassy area near a dead end street. It would take two weeks for his body to be found. Before he was shot, he and his mother had been planning his 15th birthday party.

Gunshots are the #1 cause of death of American children. Gunshots are preventable.

JANUARY 22, 2023

JORDAN NIXON
Age 17
Chicago, IL

Jordan was trying to buy a pair of sneakers from someone who claimed online to be selling a pair he liked. He set off in his car and brought some friends along for the ride. It was midday on a Sunday. After the man took his money, he failed to supply the shoes, instead shooting into the vehicle where the bullets penetrated Jordan and one of his friends. Jordan died.

TEEN
Age 15
Charlotte, NC

The boy who was shot and a 16-year-old were playing with a gun. The 16-year-old shot him. He's dead.

BRENDAN VALENZUELA
Age 15
Buckeye, AZ

Brendan was with a group of teens when trouble started up, and one of the other teens shot him. That teen and another were said to have been plotting for a week to rob Brendan. Brendan later died from his injuries.

One of the black-robed justices grabbed a pen so quickly no one saw where it came from. She scrawled, "Thoughts and prayers" across the written opinion of the highest (secular) court in the land.

Only a few hawk-eyed souls noticed the three letter logo on the pen barrel.

the end

JANUARY 23, 2023

AVA WOOD
Age 14
Baldwinsville, NY

Ava ran the fastest of all the girls on the Durgee Junior High School track team. But she couldn't outrun a bullet that entered her head while she slept. The gunman? Her father. The same father she'd adored. Ava was generous, sharing her gummies at lunch. She was a girl other kids enjoyed spending time with. She spoke of having her own kids one day so she could spoil them with love. But Ava will never have the opportunity to become a mommy. Dead from a gunshot at age 14. At the hands of a father who'd been stalking and harassing her mother.

RASHAD CARR
Age 16
Des Moines, IA

Rashad was inside the alternative school designed to keep kids out of trouble when a man armed with a 9 mm handgun came in and shot him dead. The shooter was on supervised release for weapons charges and had cut off his ankle monitor 16 minutes before Rashad's murder. The police said the shooting was part of a complicated gang dispute that saw one gang retaliating against another for a rap video Rashad had posted.

JAVIER WINSTON
Age 15
Milwaukee, WI

A few months before he died, Javier was shot in the foot. His mother warned him then to stop being friends with kids causing trouble. He didn't listen. On the day Javier died, someone followed him in a car and then shot him.

EDUARDO PRECIANO-LUEVANO
Age 17
Santa Fe, NM

Two men, aged 19 and 23, lured Eduardo to a shooting range where one of them unloaded a full clip of AK-47

Guns = inherently dangerous

When a child shoots himself with an adult family member's gun, empathy often supplants outrage. So the adult "gets away with" negligent homicide.

This would never happen were the victim not his own child.

Where's "justice" for the children?

What about deterrence?

ammunition into the teenage boy. They left his body in the driver's seat of a sedan.

JANUARY 24, 2023

DACARI GREEN
Age 16
Broken Arrow, OK

Dacari was found dead of a gunshot in front of his home. Some members of the Bloods believed he was a rat and they discussed the allegations with him on a group phone call where he was able to convince them he wasn't. However, certain gang members chose not to participate in the call and one of them, a 15-year-old girl, subsequently shot him.

> The united states of gun worship: failing our children one bloody day after another

TYCE CHESTERFIELD
Age 16
Richmond, VA

Tyce was the victim of an armed robbery committed by four juveniles. The police said the robbery was not random.

JANUARY 25, 2023

LARON HENDERSON
Age 15
Baltimore, MD

Less than an hour after dismissal from Forest Park High School in Baltimore, the six-foot-six-inch tall boy known to friends as the gentle giant was dead. Laron planned to try out for the school basketball team and eventually join the US Army. He won't be doing either.

INFORMATION IS POWER

A child dies by gunshot. Too often, police go mum. They withhold names and details to protect someone, something.

The shooter? The gun owner? The investigation? The reputation of the dead child? The gun lobby?

Names unspoken, details hidden from view. Silence facilitates repetition. Another day, another child shot dead. Another set of parents grieving.

Making names of all child gunshot death victims public as soon as kin have been notified, and making key details public within a reasonable time frame afterwards, enables the police to conduct their investigation while empowering communities to stop gun violence.

ANTHONY KRUG-OVERTON
Age 16
Toledo, OH

Anthony was a homicide victim in his West Toledo home. He died from multiple gunshot wounds. He was a teenager doing things teenagers do. And then he wasn't anymore...

> Is it a civilized country if the people stand by while the nation's children are riddled with bullets and dispatched to early graves?

CAHARI MAURICE WALTON
Age 16
Grand Rapids, MI

Cahari wanted to play football. He wanted to be a rapper. He was actively looking for a job. Now his plans will never materialize. Dead at 16 from a gunshot.

JANUARY 26, 2023

FERNANDO MARTINEZ
Age 16
Santa Rosa, TX

Fernando was shot by teens who are believed to have posed as purchasers of vaping cartridges so they could steal the cartridges. They were believed to be part of a criminal enterprise that was involved in other ripoffs that resulted in shootings. Police often refer to vape sales as "drug transactions," inadvertently casting aspersions on the teen robbery victims.

KEDDRICK TURNER
Age 13
Baton Rouge, LA

Keddrick was sitting in a car with teenagers when he was shot in the head. He died at a hospital days later.

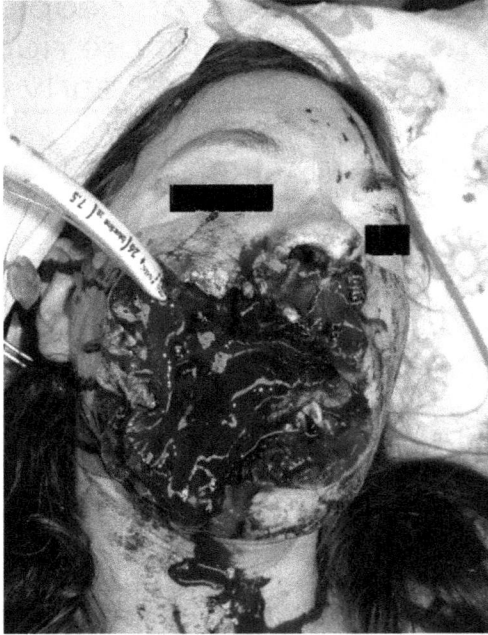

single gunshot wound to face

How many more American children will die on *your* watch before you say, "Enough!"

TY'EL HANKINS
Age 17
Kannapolis, NC

Ty'el was shot while driving a car. The police did not think the shooting was random. They arrested a 14-year-old.

JANUARY 27, 2023

MATTHEW CRUZ
Age 15
Albuquerque, NM

GABRIEL ANTONIO CRUZ
Age 14
Albuquerque, NM

Matthew and Gabriel, brothers, were both shot to death by other teens, in retaliation for the alleged theft by them of a gun belonging to the brother of one of the shooters.

TEEN
Age 17
Alexandria, VA

A group of teens were in an Alexandria hotel room on a Friday night when the unidentified 17 year old was shot by a friend. He was later pronounced dead. The friend was arrested for possessing a gun as a minor. The circumstances of the shooting haven't been released.

JANUARY 28, 2023

A'RHIANNA MOYE
Age 13
Louisville, GA

Her classmates wore her favorite pink to support her recovery as she lay wounded in the hospital for two weeks, but A'Rhianna didn't recover. She'd been shot in the neck by her older brother while visiting her

We have Federal government departments and agencies to regulate gun sales and prosecute interstate gun crimes.

We have Federal government departments and agencies to oversee public health.

We have Federal government departments and agencies that investigate products endangering children and issue recalls.

Which Federal government department or agency is tracking juvenile gun injuries and deaths?

Which Federal government department or agency was tasked with preventing the 150 children dead of avoidable gunshots in the single month January 2023 from having their bodies ripped open by bullets?

grandparents. It's uncertain whether the shooting was intentional. Her brother was charged in her death.

TYONIE ASHFORD
AGE 17
Oak Forest, IL
Tyonie was shot dead with a single gunshot. He was found at the rear of a condo building in the early afternoon.

REGINALD NEPHEW
Age 17
Pomona, CA
Reggie and his 19-year-old brother were shot at a residence in Pomona while a party was underway. Both were pronounced dead at the scene. Two years before the shooting, Reggie was featured in a news story, when he was helping out at "God's Pantry," which was described as a lifeline for needy Pomona families.

CARLOS CADENA
Age 15
Tucson, AZ
Carlos was shot dead on a bike path behind a business. Carlos himself was suspected of shooting a man January 24, and his killing may have been revenge.

BRAYDEN BOLYARD
Age 17
Austin, TX
The teen who was #8 on his high school football team and planned to go to college was at a birthday party at Ta hookah lounge when someone began shooting, and he was hit. He died. An 18-year-old was also shot and later died. Security footage showed the shooter standing on the stage, and witnesses said he was pointing a pistol at the crowd. People scrambled for the door and the shooter began shooting at the eighteen year old who died, then threw down the pistol and ran.

The 27 most misunderstood (and often deliberately misconstrued) words in the United States of America:

A well regulated Militia, being necessary to the security of a free State, the right of the people to keep and bear Arms, shall not be infringed.
U.S. Constitution, Article II

State militias can store arms in arsenals. They need not carry arms on public streets. No formal or informal state militia has children (with the exception of some 17-year-olds) as members.
Groups calling themselves militias that are not authorized by law/operated under the purview of a state government are illegal and are not protected by the Second Amendment.

JANUARY 29, 2023

KENNEDI BELTON
Age 15
New Orleans, LA

Her "best friend since birth" said Kennedi loved English classes at Warren Easton Charter High School where both were freshman. Kennedi especially likes to write. On the day of her death, she woke up at a friend's house where a group of girls were having a sleepover. A man who was a relative of the family hosting the sleepover brought a gun into the house. Police learned that he was playing with the gun when he unintentionally shot Kennedi.

> Gun-free homes save children's lives; let's trade the fantasy of keeping guns to protect children for actually protecting them by keeping guns out of their homes.

ANTHONY ALEXANDER
Age 17
Collingdale, PA

A group of people were in a residence when a 16-year-old fired a gun, killing Anthony. Anthony had been hailed as a hero just a year before his death for helping rescue 3 children who fell into an icy pond. When a log rescue wasn't working for the second child, Anthony jumped into the pond and grabbed the boy. The experience left him considering a career in law enforcement or the military. The fatal shooting was determined to have resulted from teens playing with guns. Had he lived, Anthony would have received an award for his heroism in March.

DEVON MONTGOMERY
Age 16
East St. Louis, IL

Devon and another parishioner he knew began firing guns at each other inside a church during a service, and Devon was struck by a bullet and killed.

HYSHEEN THOMAS
Age 13
Bedford, OH

Neighbors said a shooting in their neighborhood was an anomaly and they were surprised it happened. Before long, a 24-year-old shooter who'd hightailed it to Georgia was wanted on an extradition warrant. But it was too late for Hysheen who lay dying from a gunshot wound, struck as he and his brother went to a corner store for a sloppy joe for their mother. His brother was also shot but survived.

DOMINICK ALLEN
Age 17
New York, NY

Dominick Allen was shot in the chest and died after arriving at the hospital.

TYLER LAWRENCE
Age 13
Boston, MA

While visiting his grandparents on a Sunday morning, Tyler decided to take a walk. Surveillance video showed him walking along, listening to his music when a man got out of a car, spoke to him, then fired five bullets into the 13-year-old. The two had no prior connection. The shooter had a long criminal history.

JAYLEN ANDARRIUS CLARK
Age 17
Birmingham, AL

Jaylen and an 18-year-old appeared to have gotten into a physical fight with someone and were shot by that person. Jaylen died. A different 18-year-old was later charged with killing him.

JANUARY 30, 2023

CORDELL WILLIAMS
Age 13
Washington, D.C.

Cordell's family described him as a jokester, a kid who loved math at Kramer Middle School. He had an entrepreneurial spirit and would sell water bottles or pump gas to earn money when he wanted new sweatpants or t-shirts. He was with a group of friends at one of their homes when the kids came upon the gun that would end his life. The case was chalked up to playing with guns after one child pulled the trigger and a bullet entered Cordell's brain. Who might Cordell have become? We'll never know.

TEEN
Age 17
Bridgeton, NJ

A 21-year-old shot this teen boy and a 17-year-old girl. The girl survived. The boy did not. Police said it was a targeted killing and the dispute may have stemmed from something that happened at a party earlier in the day.

CARLEONE WOODLAND
Age 13
Vicksburg, MS

When Carleone was shot and killed close to midnight on a Monday night, the mayor was so steamed he put the city's children under a curfew. Three older teens were arrested in connection with the shooting.

TEEN
Age 15
Elkhart, IN

This boy's body was found outside a house after he'd been shot to death.

MARQUEZ OTIS
Age 13
Decatur, IL

Marquez liked to help his grandmother with chores and was especially enamored of spending time with his baby sister. Neither will ever see him again. Marquez, a gun, and his 16-year-old brother were in a bedroom together. Marquez didn't make it out alive. Marquez teasingly told his brother to shoot him with the gun kept in their house, and his brother checked to see that the safety was in place and pulled the trigger. The safety failed. The 16-year-old brother was arrested on an involuntary manslaughter charge. Marquez was at least the 14th American child to die in the month of January as a result of children "playing with guns."

What if instead of donating $$$$$ to "send a child off properly," i.e., buying a luxury coffin truckloads of flowers and balloons, an engraved tombstone, and a catered feast for mourners, we all spent our money to keep children alive?

What if we invested our time and our money to prevent and reverse the conditions that foster gun violence?

MONTEVIUS GOSS
Age 16
Louisville, MS

Montevious liked to write rap lyrics. He had a big smile. His favorite subject was math. He disappeared in early January and then as the month came to a close his body was found in the woods alongside a railyard. He'd been shot through the upper arm, with the bullet proceeding through his chest.

JANUARY 31, 2023

LUIS CASTRO
Age 16
Miami, FL

Luis was in the passenger seat with a 20-year-old friend at the wheel, driving in the Golden Glades neighborhood of Miami when one or more people fired guns at the car. Both were killed. Two backseat passengers survived.

DIEGO TURCIOS
Age 17
Hutto, TX

Diego and another young man were shot in Hutto, Texas in the Lakeside Estates neighborhood. Two men were charged in the case.

One month.
31 days.

150 children no longer with us, their hopes, dreams, and plans gone up in gunsmoke.
You, me, all of us adults let this happen on our watch.
We failed these kids who depended on us, their community, to keep them safe.
Isn't it time we started protecting America's children?

You can help write the end to this story.

Let's Do It!

January's Stats

The number of kids shot to death in the United States in the single month of January 2023 is 150.

The number of days this month without a fatal child shooting is ZERO.

The number of fatal child shootings per day this month ranged from 2 to 11.

The number of children intentionally murdered by a parent in this single month is 15. That's an average of one every other day.

The number of American children shot dead this month in their own, a relative's, or a friend's home, combined, is 70.
- 40 children shot in their own homes.
- 21 children shot in a relative's home.
- 9 children shot in a friend's home.

The youngest child shot to death in January 2023 was 10 months old.

21 of the children shot to death in January were less than 12 years old.

The number of children whose deaths this month were attributed to "playing with guns" was 14, with 5 possible additional cases.

17 Steps to Sanity

- Prioritize children's right to remain alive. <u>Prosecute</u> owners whose guns fall into the hands of children every time.
- Prohibit <u>use/handling</u> of guns by children under 12 without exception; for ages 12 to 18, require direct and immediate supervision by parent/guardian or licensed instructor for hunting or target shooting with assumption of legal responsibility for the child's actions.
- Bar purchases of handguns and long guns from any type of seller by anyone under age 21. Require police to confiscate and destroy any gun they encounter in the possession of a person under 21 or any person temporarily barred from gun ownership; require parents/guardians to turn in to the police for destruction any gun found by them to have come into the possession of their minor child.
- Full <u>accountability</u> for every gun death; publicly disclose names of persons dead of gunshots immediately after kin are notified and provide sufficient details reasonably soon thereafter to inform the public of the factors contributing to the death, including the identity of the gun owner.
- Where a home is legally shared, require <u>consent</u> of all adults for in-home gun storage.
- Strict liability for <u>misuse</u> - a gun is inherently dangerous by definition.
- Strict liability for sales to <u>persons barred</u> from gun ownership.
- Strict liability for manufacturers in the case of <u>defective weapons or safeties</u> causing death.
- <u>Track all gun purchases, transfers, loss, and/or destruction</u> as is done with cars.

- Mandatory use of <u>gun safes/lockers</u> for all guns when not in use and being handled directly by the owner.
- Mandate alternate location <u>gun storage</u> for households with children under 7.
- Educate divorcing couples about dealing with the stress of divorce safely. Provide for <u>temporary gun monitoring</u> during this time so strongly linked to murder of family members: require every couple filing for divorce to indicate on the divorce petition whether either party owns guns and if so, how many, what type, and where located; bar new purchases until 90 days after the divorce is final; if abuse is alleged at time of filing or during proceedings, protect the children/spouse by requiring guns to be deposited with the court until 90 days after the divorce is final. Encourage voluntary deposits.
- Require a forensic psychiatric examination by a court-appointed <u>mental health</u> professional before gun ownership rights are restored whenever the right has been temporarily removed or restricted for cause.
- Require <u>liability insurance</u> for gun owners.
- Require and provide <u>free classroom and hands-on instruction at a shooting range for all inexperienced gun purchasers</u> who have not safely owned and used a gun for at least 5 years, including lessons on the social and psychological ramifications of gun ownership and use.
- Close trade show and personal sales <u>loopholes</u>.
- Ban <u>assault weapons</u> and <u>high-capacity magazines</u>.

Sources

1. "Children Killed or Injured in 2023" Gun Violence Archive.
https://www.gunviolencearchive.org/reports/child-injured-killed?sort=asc&order=Incident%20Date.
2. Kauffman, Julia. "Family Mourns 5 Year Old Girl Killed in North Charlotte Shooting." WCNC.com. January 6, 2023.
https://www.wcnc.com/article/news/crime/5-year-old-killed-shooting-north-charlotte-family-mourns/275-bfdec91b-3ec4-4e94-a88b-39bd1adfc446.
3. Gaskins, Cam. "'It hurts so bad: Community and family hold vigil for 5-year-old killed on New Year's Day." WBTV.com. January 6, 2023.
https://www.wbtv.com/2023/01/07/it-hurts-so-bad-community-family-hold-vigil-5-year-old-shot-killed-new-years-day/
4. Hami, Eran. "Father details how 11-year-old daughter was killed by celebratory gunfire on New Year's." KRIS6News.com. January 2, 2023.
https://www.kristv.com/news/local-news/father-details-how-11-year-old-daughter-was-killed-by-celebratory-gunfire-on-new-years.
5. Struett, David. "Teen driver killed, 3 wounded, in Washington Park car-to-car shooting." Chicago Sun Times. January 1, 2023.
6. Ong, Eli and Tumulty, Brónagh. "Teen killed in shooting near Washington Park ID'd." WGNTV.com. January 1, 2023.
https://wgntv.com/news/chicagocrime/4-people-shot-near-washington-park/.
7. Matthews, Elizabeth. "New details released in Chicago shooting death of 9-year-old Jarvis Watts." Fox32Chicago.com. January 2, 2023.
https://wgntv.com/news/chicagocrime/4-people-shot-near-washington-park/.
8. "In moments after 9-year-old was fatally shot, the gun and an adult left the house, Chicago police report says." CWBChicago.com. January 3, 2023.
https://cwbchicago.com/2023/01/in-moments-after-9-year-old-was-fatally-shot-the-gun-and-an-adult-left-the-house-before-cops-arrived-chicago-police-report-says.html.
9. Gray, Shardaa and Terry, Jermont. "'I feel really bad:' police probe shooting death of 9-year-old on New Year's Day." CBSnews.com. January 2, 2023.
https://www.cbsnews.com/chicago/news/shooting-death-9-year-old/
10. Schuba, Tom. "9-year-old pointed gun at his head and killed himself in Washington Heights, witness told police." Chicago Sun Times. January 4, 2023.
https://chicago.suntimes.com/crime/2023/1/4/23539796/9-year-old-boy-pointed-gun-accidentally-shot-himself-washington-heights-home
11. Hellgren, Mike. "Loved ones mourn D'Asia Garrison, 17, Baltimore's first homicide victim of 2023. CBSnews.com. January 2, 2023.
https://www.cbsnews.com/baltimore/news/loved-ones-mourn-dasia-garrison-17-baltimores-first-homicide-victim-of-2023/
12. "26-year-old arrested and charged with 1st degree murder." Baltimore police department media release. January 23, 2023.
https://www.cbsnews.com/baltimore/news/loved-ones-mourn-dasia-garrison-17-baltimores-first-homicide-victim-of-2023/
13. "Teen killed, 2 others wounded in overnight shooting near 32nd and Villard." CBS58.com. January 2, 2023.
https://www.cbs58.com/news/teen-killed-in-overnight-shooting-wounds-two
14. Hughes, Eliot. "'Reach out, let us support you:' community members call for peace as new year begins in Milwaukee." Milwaukee Journal Sentinel. January 3, 2023.
15. Flowers, Brittany and Horak, David. "Family mourns 16-year-old killed in New Year's shooting: 'He'll be remembered.'" January 2, 2023.
https://www.woodtv.com/news/grand-rapids/family-ids-16-year-old-killed-in-new-years-day-shooting/
16. Buursma, Madalyn. "GRPD: Teen shot, killed, near celebratory New Year's gunfire." January 3, 2023.
https://www.woodtv.com/news/grand-rapids/grpd-teen-shot-killed-near-celebratory-new-years-gunfire/
17. Keller, Blake. "Police: victim identified in first murder of year." January 2, 2023.
https://www.wnem.com/2023/01/02/saginaw-police-investigating-first-murder-year/.

18. "GoFundMe started for funeral of Saginaw teen 'whose life was cut short due to senseless gun violence.'" Mlive. January 6, 2023.
https://www.mlive.com/news/saginaw-bay-city/2023/01/gofundme-started-for-funeral-of-s aginaw-teen-whose-life-was-cut-short-due-to-senseless-gun-violence.html/

19. "Mother, 6-year-old daughter killed in suspected murder-suicide inside North Harris county home, sheriff says." KRPC. January 3, 2023.
https://www.click2houston.com/news/local/2023/01/03/investigation-underway-after-woman-child-found-dead-inside-north-harris-county-home-deputies-say/

20. Ferguson, John Wayne. "Mother, daughter found dead in suspected murder-suicide near Spring." Houston Chronicle. January 3, 2023.
https://www.houstonchronicle.com/news/houston-texas/crime/article/spring-texas-shooting-woman-child-dead-17692311.php.

21. McCord, Cory. HCSO: Woman shot, killed her 6-year-old daughter before killing herself at Spring area home." KHOU.com January 3, 2023.
https://www.khou.com/article/news/local/woman-child-shot-killed-spring-texas/285-1514fc63-3f83-4fe9-8 959-f87dcdd25126

22. "Teen shot multiple times, killed in Mansfield hotel." ABC6onyourside.com. January 3, 2023.
https://abc6onyourside.com/news/local/teen-shot-multiple-times-mansfield-quality-inn

23. "Man accused of killing teen at Mansfield hotel arrested in Columbus." January 3, 2023.
https://www.10tv.com/article/news/crime/man-accused-fatally-shooting-teenage-boy-mansfield-hotel-arre sted/530-df4cf96a-040b-4a05-9c39-d63a190a9aac

24. Caudill, Mark. "Mansfield police investigating fatal shooting of teenage boy at Quality Inn." Mansfield News Journal. January 23, 2023.
https://www.mansfieldnewsjournal.com/story/news/2023/01/03/mansfield-police-investigating-fatal-shooti ng-at-quality-inn/69774456007/

25. Farrell, Brian. "17-year-old killed, 14-year-old hurt in Congress Heights metro station shooting in DC." DC News Now. January 3, 2023.
https://www.dcnewsnow.com/news/local-news/washington-dc/17-year-old-killed-14-year-old-hurt-in-cong ress-heights-metro-station-shooting-in-dc/

26. Valencia, Juliana. "17-year-old killed, 14-year-old shot at Congress Heights Metro Station: Police." NBCwashington.com. January 2, 2023.
https://www.nbcwashington.com/news/local/two-shot-at-congress-heights-metro-station-police/3245326/

27. Pope, Troy, Cremen, Alanea, and Arnold, Jess. "1 teenager killed, another injured following shooting at Congress Heights Metro station." wusa9.com. January 2, 2023.
https://www.wusa9.com/article/news/crime/congress-heights-metro-station-shooting/65-dfd9d9bb-0c88-4 148-a69e-0c66a885582c.

28. Wimbly, Randy and Komer, David. "Gunman kills himself after double murder of his cousins on Detroit's east side." Fox2detroit.com. January 2, 2023.
https://www.fox2detroit.com/news/gunman-kills-himself-after-fatally-shooting-2-people-including-teen29. Wells, Jesse. "15-year-old dies following accidental shooting." Fox59.com. January 3, 2023.
https://fox59.com/news/indycrime/15-year-old-dies-following-accidental-shooting-on-indys-east-side/

30. "'A tragedy'| teen believed to have been accidentally shot dies at hospital, IMPD says." WTHR.com. January 2, 2023.
https://www.wthr.com/article/news/local/teen-shot-east-side-of-indianapolis-dies-at-hospital/531-01963f2 a-f369-4a10-b1a4-ea7b2d76d86a

31. "Teenage boy becomes Marion County's 1st homicide victim." WRTV.com. January 2, 2023.
https://www.wrtv.com/news/local-news/crime/teenage-boy-becomes-marion-countys-first-2023-homicide-victim

32. Clemmons, Niko. "Family desperate for answers after teen shot, killed in Ft. Lauderdale." NBCmiami.com. January 6, 2023.https://www.nbcmiami.com/news/local/i-wish-this-on-nobody-family-desperate-for-answers-after-teen-shot-killed-in-fort-lauderdale/2945231/

33. Clemmons, Niko. "Family, friends hold candlelight vigil to remember teen fatally shot in Ft. Lauderdale." NBCmiami.com. January 7, 2023.
https://www.nbcmiami.com/news/local/family-friends-hold-candlelight-vigil-to-remember-teen-fatally-shot-in-fort-lauderdale/2945504/

34. Wells, Jesse. "Mistake over identical cars may have led to homicide at Castleton Square Mall"

CBS4indy.com. January 4, 2023.
https://cbs4indy.com/news/indycrime/mistake-over-identical-cars-may-have-led-to-homicide-of-16-year-o
ld-at-castleton-square-mall/
35. Crockett, Ashley. "1 teen dead, 1 injured in Monticello after Tuesday morning residential
disturbance." KATV.com. January 4, 2023.
https://katv.com/news/local/1-teen-dead-1-injured-in-monticello-after-tuesday-morning-residential-disturb
ance-drew-memorial-hospital-carlos-garcia-drew-county-southeast-arkansas-teenage-dispute-shot-succ
umbed-injuries-monticello-police-department-investigates
36. Lancaster, Grant. "Two arrested in Monticello shooting that killed 1 person, wounded another."
Arkansas Democrat Gazette. January 5, 2023.
https://www.arkansasonline.com/news/2023/jan/05/two-arrested-in-monticello-shooting-that-killed-1-pers
on-wounded-another/.
37. O'Connor, Shea. "Orleans parish coroner identifies 3 found dead in Fairgrounds home." WDSU.com.
January 25, 2023. https://www.wdsu.com/article/fairgrounds-triple-homicide-victims-identified/42659026#
38. Stunson, Mike. "16-year-old girl shot in head after refusing to pick up marijuana bag, KY cops say."
Lexington Herald Leader. January 5, 2023.
https://www.kentucky.com/news/state/kentucky/article270800692.html
39. "Man accused of killing teen because she wouldn't pick up dropped pot." Local12.com. January 3,
2023.
https://local12.com/news/local/man-accused-of-killing-teen-because-she-wouldnt-pick-up-dropped-pot-ci
ncinnati-boone-county-demarkus-hedges-scarlett-tucker-teens-burlington-silver-brook-marijuana-crime-
wanted
40. Palermo, Jill. "Dumfries kids wounded, killed in domestic shooting were grieving the recent loss of
their mother." Prince William Times. January 5, 2023.
https://www.princewilliamtimes.com/news/dumfries-kids-wounded-killed-in-domestic-shooting-were-grievi
ng-the-recent-loss-of-their-mother/article_019c4994-8d76-11ed-808f-1fa8169afc7b.html
41. Lusso, Katie. "'She was the life of the party'| Community fundraising for 3-year-old killed, siblings
injured in house shooting." WUSA9.com. January 66, 2023.
https://www.wusa9.com/article/news/local/virginia/fundraiser-dumfries-house-shooting-victims-3-year-old
-killed-siblings-hospitalized/65-014243d9-3bd2-42b8-8015-060c5538a324
42. Eberhardt, Ashley. "TCSO: father used air rifle to kill 5-year-old, himself." Fox21news.com. January
21, 2023. https://www.fox21news.com/top-stories/tcso-father-used-air-rifle-to-kill-5-year-old-himself/
43. "Father kills son in Teller County murder-suicide." CBSnews.com. January 6, 2023.
https://www.cbsnews.com/colorado/news/teller-county-florissant-william-liam-brueche-murder-suicide/
44. Soukup, Abbey. "Teller County sheriff's office defends its handling of murder-suicide involving father,
son." Pikes Peak Courier. February 1, 2023.
https://gazette.com/pikespeakcourier/teller-county-sheriffs-office-defends-its-handling-of-murder-suicide-i
nvolving-father-son/article_43f2755a-a272-11ed-a0c1-63cbf25be13e.html
45. Hellgren, Mike. "'Senseless crime:' Family pleads for justice after 16-year-old killed near Baltimore
school." CBSnews.com. January 5, 2023.
https://www.cbsnews.com/baltimore/news/senseless-crime-family-pleads-justice-baltimore-wjz-deanta-d
orsey-edmondson-village/
46. DeVoe, Annie. "Baltimore teen accused of murdering, injuring students on Popeyes lunch break."
Daily Voice. February 16, 2023.
https://dailyvoice.com/maryland/baltimore/news/baltimore-teen-accused-of-murdering-injuring-students-o
n-popeyes-lunch-break/856891/
47."17-year-old killed in shooting on Indy's near east side." WTHR.com. January 4, 2023.
https://www.wthr.com/article/news/local/1-dead-after-shooting-on-indys-near-east-side-indianapolis-india
na-ingram-street/531-6ed1f74a-3b23-4c8f-97c3-826c89c40964
48. Braden R. Wrana of Mineral City, Ohio, Obituary.
https://www.gotschallfuneralhome.com/obituary/brayden-wrana.
49. "Officials investigate shooting death of 14-year-old Mineral City boy." WJER.com. January 5, 2023.
https://www.wjer.com/news/officials-investigate-shooting-death-of-14-year-old-mineral-city-boy/
50. Miller, Jordan. "Tusky Valley remembers 14-year-old who died in accidental shooting." Jordan Miller
News. January 5, 2023.
https://www.wjer.com/news/officials-investigate-shooting-death-of-14-year-old-mineral-city-boy/

51. Fields, Christopher. "Family of 15-year-old Sha'Maya Anderson relieved her suspected killer is behind bars." WLBT.com. January 24, 2023.
https://www.wlbt.com/2023/01/25/family-15-year-old-shamaya-anderson-relieved-her-suspected-killer-is-behind-bars/
52. Ramirez, Jr., Domingo. "Fort Worth teen faces murder charges in shooting that killed 14-year-old, 17-year-old." AOL.com. February 24, 2023.
https://www.aol.com/news/fort-worth-teen-faces-murder-164417725.html
53. Tanner, Courtney. "Final report details fears and hopes of Haight family before Enoch murders." The Salt Lake Tribune." April 7, 2023.
https://www.sltrib.com/news/2023/04/07/final-report-details-fears-hopes/
54. McKellar, Katie. "Enoch mother was deemed not in 'high danger' before father killed entire Enoch family. Why?" Deseret News. April 9, 2023.
https://www.deseret.com/utah/2023/2/9/23591219/enoch-murder-suicide-domestic-violence-risk
55. Chapin, Josh. "After losing his son, Raleigh father says gun violence has to stop." ABC11.com. January 16, 2023. https://abc11.com/juvenile-crime-guns-teenagers-shot-teens-killed/12711045/
56. Bae, Cindy. "'Long live Craig': Raleigh family remembers teen killed in 'accidental' shooting." ABC11.com. January 7, 2023.
https://abc11.com/raleigh-family-remembers-craig-curtis-teen-killed-accidental-shooting/12671925/
57. Carnelius Lamar Williams, obituary. Arkansas Democrat Gazette. January 11, 2023.
https://www.arkansasonline.com/obituaries/2023/jan/11/carnelius-williams-2023-01-11/
58. Lancaster, Grant. "Victim, suspect identified in Thursday shooting in Little Rock's Mabelvale neighborhood." Arkansas Democrat Gazette. January 7, 2023.
https://www.arkansasonline.com/news/2023/jan/07/victim-suspect-identified-in-thursday-shooting-in-little-rocks-mabelvale-neighborhood/
59. Buercklin, Katie. "15-year-old boy shot and killed on Canal Street." WDSU.com. January 10, 2023.
https://www.wdsu.com/article/15-year-old-boy-shot-killed-canal-street/42433563
60. Bond, Kylee. "Teen with several gunshot wounds dies after being dropped off at hospital, NOPD says." WGNO. com. January 5, 2023.
https://wgno.com/news/crime/teen-with-several-gunshot-wounds-dies-after-being-dropped-off-at-hospital-nopd-says/
61. Kelley, Ingrid and Ainsworth, Amber. "16-year-old killed, 11-year-old hurt while playing Uno in Detroit home." fox2detroit.com. January 6, 2023.
https://www.fox2detroit.com/news/16-year-old-killed-11-year-old-hurt-in-drive-by-shooting-while-playing-uno-in-detroit-home
62. Counts, Chris. "North Little Rock police investigating deadly shooting on Pike Avenue." Kark.com. January 6, 2023.
https://www.kark.com/crime/north-little-rock-police-investigating-shooting-on-pike-avenue-1-injured/
63. "2 teens shot, 1 fatally near gas station on Chicago's west side." January 6, 2023.
https://www.gunviolencearchive.org/sites/default/files/source-screenshots/Screenshot%202023-01-06%20at%2020-41-53%202%20teens%20shot%201%20fatally%20near%20gas%20station%20on%20Chicago%27s%20West%20Side.png
64. Terry, Jermont. "West side gas station shooting leaves 1 teen dead, 1 critically injured." CBSnews.com. January 6, 2023.
https://www.cbsnews.com/chicago/news/west-side-gas-station-shooting/
65. "Teen confesses to shooting." Odessa American. January 10, 2023.
https://www.oaoa.com/local-news/teen-confesses-to-shooting/.
66. "'We are all broken:' women planned to leave partner before he killed her, their daughters." Mlive.com. January 9, 2023.
https://www.mlive.com/news/kalamazoo/2023/01/we-are-all-broken-woman-planned-to-leave-partner-before-he-killed-her-their-daughters.html
67. Krafcik, Mike. "Victim of apparent triple homicide tried to end relationship, sheriff says." WWMT.com. January 9, 2023.
https://wwmt.com/news/local/allegan-county-murder-suicide-autumn-mackenzie-hagger-roger-cindy-clouse-fennville-fatal-shooting-police-investigation

68.Lybrand, Holmes and Salaheih, Nouran. "DC man charged in shooting death of 13-year-old." CNN.com. February 1, 2023.
https://www.cnn.com/2023/02/01/us/washington-dc-karon-blake-shooting/index.html
69.Cremen, Alanea. "'I am only 12'| Warrant gives new details into shooting death of Karon Blake." WUSA9.com. January 31, 2023.
https://www.wusa9.com/article/news/local/dc/warrant-gives-new-details-into-shooting-death-of-karon-bla ke/65-f180addb-18c3-435c-b711-260fbfae8e29
70.Hermann, Peter, Duggan, Paul, and Alexander, Keith L. "D.C. man charged with killing 13 year old he said was breaking into cars." The Washington Post. January 31, 2023.
https://www.washingtonpost.com/dc-md-va/2023/01/31/karon-blake-shooting-suspect-charged/
71.Propper, David "North Carolina father killed wife, 3 kids in murder-suicide: cops." New York Post. January 9, 2023.
72. Harris, Karringtan. "Family of Highpoint murder-suicide victims release statement." Wfmynews2.com. January 18, 2023.
https://www.wfmynews2.com/article/news/local/high-point-murder-suicide-victims-family-releases-statem ent/83-39a8af53-80a0-4e8a-9ef7-2f75e3555422
73.JoVonn, Jeroslyn. "Tragedy: North Carolina father kills wife, 3 children in murder- suidice attack." Black Enterprise. January 11. 2023.
https://www.blackenterprise.com/north-carolina-father-family-of-five-tragedy/
74. Feliciano, Cristina. "17-year-old killed in North Columbus shooting." WRBI.com. January 8, 2023.
https://www.wrbl.com/news/crime/update-17-year-old-killed-in-shooting-in-north-columbus/
75. "Funeral Cost." GoFundMe. https://www.gofundme.com/f/af4d4-funeral-cost.
77. Lofaso, Britt. "Family, friends remember slain teen at New iberia candlelight vigil." KLFY.com. January 11, 2023.
https://www.klfy.com/local/iberia-parish/family-friends-remember-slain-teen-at-new-iberia-candlelight-vigil /
78.Ortique, Darcy. "Communiy gathers in New iberia following second homicide of the year." KATC.com. January 17, 2023.
79. Brown, Martha Rose. "Santee shooting victim identified." The Times and Democrat." January 9, 2023.
https://thetandd.com/news/local/santee-shooting-victim-identified/article_3afde33d-af6d-575f-9166-178f9 5949493.html
80. "Homicide detedtives investigating Saturday morning gunfire that fatally woulnded teen." Metropoltan Nashville Police Department media release. January 9,
2023.https://www.nashville.gov/departments/police/news/homicide-detectives-investigating-saturday-mor ning-gunfire-fatally-wounded-teen
80. Fiscus, Kirsten. "Nashville police investigating after 16-year-old dies following shooting, crash into IHOP." The Tennessean. January 9, 2023.
https://www.tennessean.com/story/news/crime/2023/01/09/nashville-police-investigating-teen-shot-crash -car-into-ihop/69791307007/
81.McGee, Nikki. "Family says goodbye toIHOP teen shooting victim." WKRN.com. January 9, 2023.
https://www.wkrn.com/news/local-news/nashville/family-says-goodbye-to-ihop-teen-shooting-victim/
82. "17-year-old boy in Mercer county dies after shooting." WtAE.com. January 8, 2023.
https://www.wtae.com/article/17-year-old-boy-in-mercer-county-dies-after-shooting/42425874#
83. Cloutier, Abigail. "Sharon community mourns 17-year-old homicide victim." WKB.,com. January 9, 2023. https://www.wkbn.com/news/local-news/sharon-community-mourns-17-year-old-homicide-victim/
84.Gavin David Beighley obituary. The Sharon Herald.
https://obituaries.sharonherald.com/obituary/gavin-beighley-1086957147
84. https://www.gunviolencearchive.org/incident/2500496.
85. Salcedo, Angelina, "Tampa family calls for accountability after 12-year-old shot and killed." WTSP.com. January 10, 2023.
https://www.wtsp.com/article/news/local/hillsboroughcounty/tampa-family-calls-for-accountability-12-year -old-shot-killed/67-e7aa44c7-d4c3-4255-bfea-6f92663bb5ec
86.Marrero, Tony. "Tampa family awaits answers in fatal shooting of boy, 12." Tampa Bay Times. January 20, 2023.
https://www.tampabay.com/news/tampa/2023/01/20/tampa-family-awaits-answers-fatal-shooting-boy-12/

87. Khabir Bachell Holmes obituary. Goldsboro Daily News. January 8, 2023.
https://www.goldsborodailynews.com/2023/01/17/khabir-bachell-holmes/
88. Donovan, Chelsea. "Balloon release will be held for 14-year-old boy killed near Goldsboro playground." WRAL.com. January 8, 2023.
https://www.wral.com/story/balloon-release-will-be-held-for-14-year-old-boy-killed-near-goldsboro-playground/20663033/
89."Teen found dead with multiple gunshot wounds in Jackson." WLBT.com. January 9, 2023.
https://www.wlbt.com/2023/01/10/teen-found-dead-with-multiple-gunshot-wounds-jackson/
90. Howell, Kaitlin. "Jackson teen killed in shooting on Wabash Street." WJTV.com. January 10, 2023.
https://www.wjtv.com/news/local-news/jackson-police-investigate-fatal-shooting-on-wabash-street/
91. "Families say teens have no gang affiliations after deadly shooting in Dinuba." KMPH.com. January 11,2023.
https://kmph.com/news/local/families-say-teens-have-no-gang-affiliation-after-deadly-shooting-in-dinuba
92. Reavy, Pat and Ashcraft, Emily. "17-year-old boyfriend of Piute High student charged as adult with killing her." KSL.com. January 13, 2023.
https://www.ksl.com/article/50556694/17-year-old-boyfriend-of-piute-high-student-charged-as-an-adult-with-killing-her
93. Jacqueline Nunez-Millian obituary.
https://www.maglebymortuary.com/obituaries/jackeline-nunez-millan
94. "Teen dies from multiple gunshot wounds after friends mistakenly take him to assisted living facility, police say." KSAT.com. January 11, 2023.
https://www.ksat.com/news/2023/01/11/teen-dies-from-multiple-gunshot-wounds-after-friends-mistakenly-take-him-to-assisted-living-facility-police-say/
95.Spoerre, Anna. ""A beautiful sweet soul:" Kansas City's second murder victim of 2023 was 16 years old. Kansas City Star. January 17, 2023.
https://www.kansascity.com/news/local/article271287212.html
96. Amir M. Moore obituary. https://www.serenitymemorialkc.com/obituary/Amir-MooreMartin
97.Farberov, Snajana. Baby girl, 9-year-old boy shot dead during Mississippi hostage situation." New York Post. January 10,
2023.https://nypost.com/2023/01/10/baby-averi-jones-9-year-old-boy-shot-dead-during-standoff/
98. Lambre, Jerry. ""He put a pillow over her head and shot her.:' Two young children shot to death following hostage situation in Mississippi aparment; suspect arrested." Law and Crime. January 9. 2023.
https://lawandcrime.com/crime/he-put-a-pillow-over-her-head-and-shot-her-two-young-children-shot-to-death-following-hostage-situation-in-mississippi-apartment-suspect-arrested/
99.Tiamoyo Harris, Taylor. "Man shot dead inside vehicle in Ferguson." St Louis Post-Dispatch. January 10, 2023.
https://www.stltoday.com/news/local/crime-and-courts/man-shot-dead-inside-vehicle-in-ferguson/article_ff570d98-899a-5692-b4f0-78fe88ac232a.html?_gl=1*lag2ya*_ga*NDQ3OTU4NjQ3LjE2ODQ2MzUwODE.*_ga_LCNYTE04MR*MTY4NDYzNTA4MS4xLjEuMTY4NDYzNjM4OS42MC4wLjA.#_ga=2.40567202.1247535581.1684635081-447958647.1684635081
100. "Police arrest suspect in connection with deadly shooting of 16-year-old at OKC home." KOCO.com. January 12, 2023.
https://www.koco.com/article/oklahoma-city-deadly-shooting-teenager-killed-suspect-arrested/42476487
101. Pierce, Jennifer. "17-year-old shooting victim's mother speaks out after suspect arrested." Mewson6.com. January 12, 2023.
102 "Neighbor concerned after 15-year-old found shot, killed in south Macon." 13WMAZ.com. January 10, 2023.
https://www.13wmaz.com/article/news/crime/i-can-only-imagine-what-the-mother-is-going-through-neighbor-concerned-after-15-year-old-shot-killed-in-south-macon-2/93-1872b110-f3a7-45d2-94c6-f4239ec7a6ad
103. Greenwald, Joy. "Cheyene shooting victim had dreams of being an attorney or cosmetologist." WGAB.com.
https://kgab.com/cheyenne-shooting-victim-had-dreams-of-being-an-attorney-or-cosmetologist/.
104. Mcfarland, Clair." Cheyenne teens charged with killing 16-year-old have until March 20 to reach plea" March 15, 2023. Cowboy State Daily.

https://cowboystatedaily.com/2023/03/15/cheyenne-teens-charged-with-killing-16-year-old-girl-have-until-march-30-to-reach-plea/
105. "Teen killed in Hopewell, shooting suspects caught." NBC12.com. January 10, 2023
106. Childress, Autumn. "17-year-old shot, killed in Hopewell, police say." WRIC.xom. January 10, 2023.
https://www.wric.com/news/local-news/the-tri-cities/17-year-old-shot-killed-in-hopewell-police-say/
107.Stewart, Steve. "Community mourns death of Pineland teenager." Hemphill Daily News & More. January 16, 2023.
http://www.dailynewsandmore.com/lifestyle/community-mourns-death-of-pineland-teenager/article_2f1736d4-9070-11ed-adba-3be82140d601.html
108. VanHelst, Megan. "Police have suspect in fatal shooting of teen in Wildomar." Patch. January 13, 2023.
https://patch.com/california/lakeelsinore-wildomar/search-killer-ongoing-after-teen-fatally-shot-wildomar-report
109. Chow, Vivian. "16-year-old boy fatally shot in Riverside County, authorities investigating." KTLA.com. January 19, 2023.
https://ktla.com/news/local-news/16-year-old-boy-fatally-shot-in-riverside-county-authorities-investigating/
110. "Shane Hamilton killed:person of interest Kayleb Garfield in custody but not charged in teen's death." ABC13.com. January 20, 2023.
https://abc13.com/shane-hamilton-killed-star-baytown-athlete-murder-kayleb-garfield-arrest-kaleb/12721627/
111.Turner, Re'Chelle. "Family praying for justice after 16-year-old was gunned down outside Baytown apartment." Click2Houston.com. January 14, 2023.
https://www.click2houston.com/news/local/2023/01/14/family-praying-for-justice-after-16-year-old-was-gunned-down-outside-baytown-apartment/
112."Teen killed in attempted robbery moments after walking out of DeKalb gas station, mother says." WSBTV.com. January 10, 2023.
https://www.wsbtv.com/news/local/teen-killed-attempted-robbery-moments-after-walking-out-dekalb-gas-station-mother-says/ZBQSIDIT3NE6JKRNJ5KK2GQUFE/
113.Rooney, Caitlin. "Teenager arrested over shooting death of another teen in Central Lubbock, LPD said." EverythingLubbock.com. January 12, 2023,
https://www.everythinglubbock.com/news/local-news/teenager-arrested-over-shooting-death-of-another-teen-in-central-lubbock-lpd-said/
114.Tomczuk,Jack. "Detectives looking to identify gunmen who killed teen in North Philadelphia." MetroPhiladelphia.com. February 15, 2023.
https://metrophiladelphia.com/north-philadelphia-teen-homicide-video/
115. Petrillo, Matt. "New surveillance video released in Tioga fatal shooting of teen." CBSnews.com. February 15, 2023.
https://www.cbsnews.com/philadelphia/news/tioga-16-year-old-boy-fatal-shooting-surveillance-video-suspects-wanted/.
116. Whitley, Morgan. "Teen charged as adult in 16-year-old girl's death."KDVR.com. January 23, 2023.
https://kdvr.com/news/local/teen-being-charged-as-adult-in-16-year-old-girls-death/
117.Lopez, Kristian. " Sister of teen fatally shot in Denver describes moments suspect approached them, forever shattered her life." Denver7.com. January 15, 2023.
https://www.denver7.com/news/local-news/sister-of-teen-fatally-shot-in-denver-describes-moments-suspect-approached-them-forever-shattered-her-life
118. Arenas, Jasmine. "Family mourns loss of 16-year-old, wants suspect to come forward." CBSnews.com. January 13, 2023.
https://www.cbsnews.com/colorado/news/family-mourns-loss-16-year-old-wants-suspect-come-forward/
119. Isenberg, Sydney. "Juvenile arrested after teen girl shot, killed in Denver's Montbello neighborhood." Denver7.com. January 13, 2023.
120. "16-year-old shot, killed during drug deal gone wrong in Denver's Montebello neighborhood." CBSColorado.com. January 23, 2023.
121. "My Firstborn and Only Son (Xaviar Siess)." GoFundMe.

122. Dowling, Jennifer. "Family of Tacoma student killed near bus stop says he 'loved everybody." Fox13Seattle.com. January 13, 2023.
https://www.fox13seattle.com/news/family-says-tacoma-student-killed-near-bus-stop-loved-everybody
123. Horne, Deborah. "17-year-old suspect in Tacoma teen's murder appears in court." KIRO7. January 18, 2023. https://www.yahoo.com/now/17-old-suspect-tacoma-teen-051211248.html
124. Lepp, Mike and Adams, Richard. "13-year-old Jefferson County shooting victim, A'Rhianna Moye, dies." WJBF.com. January 30, 2023.
https://www.wjbf.com/news/crime-news/13-year-old-jefferson-county-shooting-victim-arhianna-moye-dies
/
125. "13-year-old Georgia girl dies after police say she was shot by her own brother." WSBradio.com. January 31, 2023.
https://www.wsbradio.com/news/local/13-year-old-georgia-girl-dies-after-police-say-she-was-shot-by-her-own-brother/VFG2UQAO6VATPC7YHMYRMRX7BE/
126. Dortch, Winnie. "Loved ones shocked after Cleveland family slain in shooting:'there were no signs.'" Cleveland19.com. January 16,
2023. https://www.cleveland19.com/2023/01/16/loved-ones-shocked-after-cleveland-family-slain-shooting-there-were-no-signs/
127. "4th victim dies following shooting on Cleveland's West Side, suspect charged." Cleveland19.com. January 13, 2023.
https://www.cleveland19.com/2023/01/14/5-people-shot-clevelands-brooklyn-centre-neighborhood-police-say/
128. Charles County Sheriff's Office press release. "Suspect in shooting and murder of Westlake HIgh School student identified and apprehended." January 19, 2023.
https://www.ccso.us/press-releases/11916/
129. Failla, Zak. "Teen killed while walking home in Waldorf nieghborhood, sheriff says." Daily Voice. January 14, 2023.
https://dailyvoice.com/maryland/charles/police-fire/teen-killed-while-walking-home-in-charles-county-neighborhood-sheriff-says/854249/
130. "Police identify teenager fatally shot in North Minneapolis." CBSnews.com January 19.
https://www.cbsnews.com/minnesota/news/police-identify-teenager-fatally-shot-in-north-minneapolis/
131. Dwyane Scott Dzubay Percy obituary.
https://www.chilsonfuneralhome.com/dwayne-scott-dzubay-percy-dweezy/
132. "Man accused of driving shooter in North Minneapolis homicide." KSTP.com. January 28, 2023.
https://kstp.com/kstp-news/local-news/man-accused-of-driving-shooter-in-north-minneapolis-homicide/
133. Graves, Kye. " Teen victim, suspect identified in West Phoenix shooting." Arizona Republic. January 17, 2023.
https://www.azcentral.com/story/news/local/phoenix-breaking/2023/01/17/18-year-old-identified-as-suspect-in-fatal-west-phoenix-shooting/69815287007/
134. "Gas station employee arrested in Phoenix shooting that left teen dead, police say." FOx10phoenix.com. January 15, 2023.
https://www.fox10phoenix.com/news/phoenix-shooting-leaves-child-critically-injured
135. Krinjak, Jon. "Family struggling to process why father and son were murdered in Llano County." Fox7Austin.com. January 16, 2023.
136. Robinson, Carol. "17-year-old identified as victim found shot to death in backyard of Birmingham home." AL.com. January 16, 2023.
https://www.al.com/news/birmingham/2023/01/17-year-old-identified-as-victim-found-shot-to-death-in-back-yard-of-birmingham-house.html
137. Leach, Olivia. "Let this save somebody else's child:" Mom of killed DeSoto boy hopes his death serves as lesson." CBSNews.com. January 16, 2023.
https://www.cbsnews.com/texas/news/let-this-save-somebody-elses-child-mom-killed-desoto-boy-hopes-death-serves-lesson/
138. Fernandez, Dermond. "'Protect your babies:' family of 11-year-old boy fatally shot in Dallas calls for peace." WFAA.com. January 16, 2023.
https://www.wfaa.com/article/news/local/dallas-police-11-year-old-shot-at-apartment-complex-family-speaks/287-a6cc7129-abea-4771-81ff-32dec6126899

139. Wessell, Todd. "Police may be closing in on suspect in killing of teen in Des Plaines." Journal & Topics. January 17, 2023. https://www.journal-topics.com/articles/police-may-be-closing-in-on-suspect-in-killing-of-teen-in-des-plaines/

140. Waldroup, Regina. "'People know more than they are saying" mother of teen shot in suburb insists." NBCChicago.com. January 16, 2023. https://www.nbcchicago.com/news/local/people-know-more-than-they-are-saying-mother-of-teen-shot-and-killed-in-suburb-insists/3046726/

141. Wessell, Todd. "Was Des Plaines just a meet-up point before killing?" Journal & Topics May 10, 2023. https://www.journal-topics.com/articles/was-des-plaines-just-a-meet-up-point-before-killing/

142. "Family identifies 16-year-old shot while driving in Tacoma; suspect info sought." Fox13Seattle.com. January 31, 2023. https://www.fox13seattle.com/news/tacoma-police-looking-for-info-suspects-in-deadly-shooting-of-16-year-old

143. Mayes, Jamie. "Family of 14-year-old killed in Wyandotte shooting says they're unsure if it was intentional." WLKY.com. January 16, 2023. https://www.wlky.com/article/family-14-year-old-killed-wyandotte-shooting-says-unsure-intentional-louisville-javarius-hendrix/42526086#

144. Lally, Tom. "Louisville mother describes what happend the day her son was shot, killed." WHAS11.com. January 16, 2023https://www.whas11.com/article/news/local/wyandotte-shooting-sunday-javarius-terese-hendrix-louisville-kentucky/417-abe2cf16-0107-4f56-924e-2bf8222d6f72

145. Glenn, Teyah. "12-year-old identified in Winston-Salem double shooting." WFMYnews.com. January 18, 2023. https://www.wfmynews2.com/article/news/crime/police-identify-12-year-old-girl-shot-and-killed-in-double-shooting-at-winston-salem-park/83-5afa5785-2738-4be9-8dd2-dbdbb4252c3e

146. "Two teens, one man identified after fatal shooting Sunday in Rockford." WIFR.com. January 17, 2023. https://www.wifr.com/2023/01/17/two-teens-one-man-identified-after-fatal-shooting-sunday-rockford/

147. "One suspect in custody after 23rd Street shooting in Rockford." WIFRcom. January 17, 2023. https://www.wifr.com/2023/01/17/one-suspect-custody-after-23rd-street-shooting-rockford/

148. Hayes, Ann and Stevenson, Darian. "How Syracuse police made arrests in murder of 11-year-old Brexialee in 10 days." Syracuse.com. January 31, 2023. https://www.syracuse.com/crime/2023/01/how-syracuse-police-made-arrests-in-the-murder-of-11-year-old-brexialee-in-10-days.html

149. Brexialee "Brexi" A. Torres-Ortiz obituary. https://memoriesfuneralhome.com/tribute/details/1037/Brexialee-Torres-Ortiz/obituary.html

150. "2-year-old boy reportedly shot dead while riding in vehicle in central Alabama." AL.com. January 17, 2023. https://www.al.com/news/montgomery/2023/01/2-year-old-boy-reportedly-shot-dead-while-riding-in-vehicle-in-central-alabama.html

151. "Toddler shot, killed in Wilcox County." WAKA.com. January 17, 2023. https://www.waka.com/2023/01/17/toddler-shot-killed-in-wilcox-county/

152. "Police" 16-year-old found in Oak Cliff creek was was murdered by 22-year-old boyfriend." WFAA.com. January 23, 2023. https://www.wfaa.com/article/news/local/venus-rodriguez-arturo-flores-oak-cliff-creek-dallas-murder-jan-16-2023/287-56c69313-f044-4f07-b6ea-a3f901169597

153. Yorgey, Tori.``13-year-old boy in custody in shooting death of another 13-year-old in Clairton." WTAE.com. January 18, 2023.https://www.wtae.com/article/clairton-wilson-avenue-police-investigation/42527071

154. James. Sarafina. "'A tragedy no one was prepared for:' Vigil held for 13-year-old boy shot, killed in Clairton." WPXI.com. January 18, 2023. https://www.wpxi.com/news/local/tragedy-no-one-was-prepared-vigil-held-13-year-old-boy-shot-killed-clairton/J42SRN2EXRBUPMQ3KAG36QCCYM/

155. Hawkins, Brian. "Suspect on the run after shooting kills two teens in Gainsville, police say." WFAA.com. January 17, 2023.

https://www.wfaa.com/article/news/crime/gainesville-texas-tx-shooting-culberson-street-us-highway-82-monday-january-16-2023/287-c5c106c6-0c16-4283-9261-1c1b9e4687eb

156.Cluiss-Fletcher, Caroline and KXII staff. "1 man, 1 teen dead after Gainesville shooting." KXII.com. January 17, 2023. https://www.kxii.com/2023/01/17/1-man-1-teen-dead-after-gainesville-shooting/

157. Oliver, Joey. "Flint homicide victim 'made an impact on everyone he met,' mother says." Mlive.com. February 10, 2023.
https://www.mlive.com/news/flint/2023/02/flint-homicide-victim-made-an-impact-on-everyone-he-met-mother-says.html

158. Cordarian DeShawn Hall obituary.
https://www.terrellbroadyfuneralhome.com/obituaries/cordarion-hall

159. Wright, Lucas. "14-year-old victim dies days after North Nashville shooting." WKRN.com. January 20, 2023.
https://www.wkrn.com/news/local-news/nashville/14-year-old-victim-dies-days-after-north-nashville-shooting/

160. Johnson, Dionne. "Juvenile victim in Crowley shooting has died." Klfy.com. January 18, 2023.
https://www.klfy.com/local/acadia-parish/juvenile-in-critical-condition-after-shooting-in-crowley/

161. Navarro, Elisa. "Suspect pleads not guilty in Goshen shooting that killed 6, second remains in hospital." ABC30.com. February 8, 2023.
https://abc30.com/goshen-shooting-six-people-killed-mother-and-baby-shot-central-california-tulare-county-massacre/12781591/

162. "6 victims of 'cartel-style execution,' including teen and baby identified." ABC7news.com. January 18, 2023. https://abc7news.com/goshen-california-shooting-ca-in-tulare/12712901/

163. McPhee, Michele. "EXCLUSIVE: Likely target of massacre was arrested hours before murder." Los Angeles Magazine. February 13, 2023.
https://www.lamag.com/citythinkblog/exclusive-goshen-massacre-gang-rival-target-left-home-ahead-of-killings/

164. Oscar Beck obituary. https://memorials.fairhavenfortwayne.com/oscar-beck/5124914/

165. Paras, Andy. "Ft. Wayne mother killed her 7-year-old son, then herself." WFFT.com. January 19, 2023.
https://www.wfft.com/news/police-fort-wayne-mother-killed-7-year-old-son-then-herself/article_7ffa0a64-9817-11ed-9905-5391e5524f2e.html

166."UPDATE: Man who allegedly murdered his children in Murfreesboro reportedly killed his wife in Alabama approximately 2 months ago." WGNSradio.com. January 19, 2023.
https://www.wgnsradio.com/article/79051/update-man-who-allegedly-murdered-his-children-in-murfreesboro-reportedly-killed-his-wife-in-alabama-approximately-2-months-ago

167. "UPDATE: Investigation into murder/suicide involving 2 children and their father in Murfreesboro." WGNSradio.com. January 26, 2023.
https://www.wgnsradio.com/article/79179/update-investigation-into-murder-suicide-involving-2-children-and-their-father-in-murfreesboro

168. Thornton, William. "Alabama mother of 2 boys killed by father was beaten to death." AL.com. February 1, 2023.
https://www.wgnsradio.com/article/79179/update-investigation-into-murder-suicide-involving-2-children-and-their-father-in-murfreesboro

169. Kelly, Mark and Guerry, Colleen. "Middle TN racing community remembers AL family killed in murder-suicide." WKRN.com. January 20, 2023.
https://www.wkrn.com/news/local-news/murfreesboro/middle-tn-racing-community-remembers-al-family-killed-in-murder-suicide/

169. "UPDATE: Two booked in shooting death of 5-year-old." KATC.com. January 20, 2023.
https://www.katc.com/news/jeff-davis-parish/update-two-booked-in-shooting-death-of-five-year-old

170. "16-year-old boy shot and killed in Wasco identified." Bakersfield Now. February 23, 2023.
https://bakersfieldnow.com/news/local/16-year-old-boy-shot-and-killed-in-wasco-identified

171. "16-year-old dies after triple shooting in Frankford: police." CBSNews.com. January 19, 2023.
https://www.cbsnews.com/philadelphia/news/sixteen-year-old-boy-dies-triple-shooting-frankford-philadelphia/

172. Lum, Justin, Phan, May and Corrado, Brent. "Teen girl dies after Coolidge drive-by shooting; 4 suspects arrested." Fox10Phoenix.com. January 20 2023.
https://www.fox10phoenix.com/news/teen-girl-dies-after-coolidge-drive-by-shooting-killer-on-the-loose
173. Loya, Adriana. "'Bubbly, energtic, family-oriented:' family remembers 14-year-old killed in Coolidge drive-by shooting." 12News.com. January, 20, 2023.
https://www.12news.com/article/news/local/arizona/family-of-14-year-old-killed-in-coolidge-home-remember-her-and-seek-justice/75-4edc628f-8cf2-4408-ab1e-fd74a00ebd63
174. Basu, Malini. "'He was my rock': Mother of 17-year-old killed outside Fort Worth Whataburger speaks out." WFAA.com. January 22, 2023.
https://www.wfaa.com/article/news/local/fort-worth-whataburger-shooting-zechariah-trevino-paschal-high-school/287-83d125c5-7f79-427d-a7f5-50247c4ed46e
175. Suarez, Miranda. "They're moms who lost children to gun violence in North Texas, and are now taking action." KERANews.org. March 21, 2023.
https://www.wfaa.com/article/news/local/fort-worth-whataburger-shooting-zechariah-trevino-paschal-high-school/287-83d125c5-7f79-427d-a7f5-50247c4ed46e
176. "Man arrested in Charlotte in connection with NY shooting that killed teen." WBTV.com. March 8, 2023.
https://www.wbtv.com/2023/03/09/man-arrested-east-charlotte-after-killing-teen-injuring-another-new-york-shooting/
177. Yu, Janice and Eyewitness News. "15-year-old boy dies after being shot in head outside rec center in the Bronx." ABC7NewYork.com. January 20, 2023.
https://abc7ny.com/bronx-teens-shot-nyc-crime-shooting/12720642/
178. Donlevy, Katherine. "Teen convicted of 2021 hit-and-run of mom and baby killed in California shooting." New York Post. January 20, 2023.
https://nypost.com/2023/01/20/la-teen-that-ran-over-mom-baby-in-21-shot-to-death/
179. "Five charges in fatal shooting of 17-year-old in Darlington." WMBFnews.com. January 20, 2023.
https://www.wmbfnews.com/2021/02/19/five-charged-fatal-shooting-year-old-darlington/
180. White, Dawn. "'Tears won't stop until I get justice:' family of 13-year-old says he was innocent bystander of gun violence." 11alive.com. January 24, 2023.
https://www.11alive.com/article/news/crime/family-13-year-old-deshon-dubose/85-6221f53b-c816-46ea-80e5-5859199ed234
181. Robinson, Carol. "Authorities ID 12-year-old boy who died in weekend Jefferson County shooting." AL.com. January 23, 2023.
https://www.al.com/news/birmingham/2023/01/authorities-id-12-year-old-boy-who-died-in-weekend-jefferson-county-shooting.html
182. Money, Joney. "Update on Juvenile Fatality." Sheriff's Office, Jefferson County, AL. January 23, 2023. https://jeffcosheriffal.com/update-on-juvenile-fatality/
183. "Teen charged in shooting death of 14-year-old boy." CBS58.com. January 27, 2023.
https://www.cbs58.com/news/teen-charged-in-shooting-death-of-14-year-old-boy#:~:text=Police%20say%2014%2Dyear%2Dold,result%20of%20multiple%20gunshot%20wounds.
184. "14-year-old 'playing with' gun killed teen, injured brother: complaint." Fox6now.com. January 26, 2023. https://www.fox6now.com/news/milwaukee-fatal-shooting-teen-accused-52nd-clarke
185. "14-year-old charged with shooting, killing 14-year-old, injuring another teen." WISN.com. January 26, 2023.
https://www.wisn.com/article/14-year-old-charged-with-shooting-killing-14-year-old-injuring-another-teen/42678599
186. Davis, John W. "Ceremony for Khalil Saleem, former Lakewood athlete killed in shooting, includes gift from Navy football program." Press-Telegram. February 11, 2023.
https://www.presstelegram.com/2023/02/11/ceremony-for-khalil-saleem-former-lakewood-athlete-killed-in-shooting-includes-gift-from-navy-football-program/
187. Anaya-Morga, Laura."'He was just playing basketball': Family mourns Long Beach teen killed in drive-by shooting." Long Beach Post News. January 27, 2023.
https://lbpost.com/news/news/he-was-just-playing-basketball-family-mourns-long-beach-teen-killed-in-drive-by-shooting/
188. Gessler, Paul. "'They took my baby':Baltimore community mourns death of 10th-grade student to gun violence." CBSnews.com. January 22, 2023.

https://www.cbsnews.com/baltimore/news/they-took-my-baby-baltimore-county-community-mourns-death-of-10th-grade-student-to-gun-violence/
189. Styles, Kat. "150 year-old usher at Morningstar Baptist Church of Christ fatally shot." Crossmap News.
https://cities.crossmap.com/dc/news/15-year-old-usher-at-morning-star-baptist-church-of-christ-fatally-shot-Ok8jRDnSq9
190. https://twitter.com/Killmoenetwork/status/1616949468229672966
191. "Investigation into male found deceased at 2000 Firnat Street." Houston Police Dept. February 6, 2023. https://www.houstontx.gov/police/nr/2023/feb/nr230206-2.htm
192. "Missing Houston boy Carlos Lugo found dead in field on Firnat St." Fox26.Houston.com. February 26, 2023.
https://www.fox26houston.com/news/missing-houston-boy-carlos-lugo-found-dead-shooting-field-firnat
193. "Chicago Shooting: Man charged with fatal shooting of teen trying to buy sneakers in West Pullman." ABC7Chicago.com. January 26, 2023.
194. "Teen killed in West Pullman shooting while trying to buy sneakers ID'd; second teen wounded." ABC7Chicago.com. January 23, 2023.
https://abc7chicago.com/chicago-shooting-teen-shot-killed-buying-sneakers/12726934/
195. Donovan, Evan and Counts, Glenn. "16-year-old charged after teen shot, killed in Charlotte, CMPD says." WSOCTV.com. January 23, 2023.
https://www.wsoctv.com/news/local/homicide-investigation-underway-east-charlotte-cmpd-says/4ZMQHPV44RGYHOCJU6C6XOBQ2U/
196. Mittower, Abby. "Police: 15-year-old killed while playing with a gun in East Charlotte." WCCBCharlotte.com. January 23, 2023.
https://www.wccbcharlotte.com/2023/01/23/cmpd-investigating-a-homicide-in-east-charlotte/
197. Sepulveda, Laura Daniella. "Teenager arrested in shooting death of 15-year-old in Buckeye." Arizona Republic. February 6,
2023.https://www.azcentral.com/story/news/local/2023/02/06/buckeye-teen-arrested-after-death-of-15-year-old-brendan-valenzuela/69875250007/
198. "2nd suspect arrested in shooting death of 15-year-old in Buckeye." AZFamily.com. March 16, 2023.https://www.azfamily.com/2023/03/16/2nd-suspect-arrested-shooting-death-15-year-old-buckeye/
199. Acosta, Nicole. "Man told estranged wife, "This is how it ends for us." The next day, he killed their daughter in murder-suicide." People.com. January 24, 2023.
https://people.com/crime/14-year-old-girl-killed-father-apparent-murder-suicide/
200. Steinbuch, Yaron. "Christopher Wood bought shotgun 16 days before killing daughter in murder-suicide." New York Post, January 25, 2023.
https://nypost.com/2023/01/25/ny-dad-bought-shotgun-16-days-before-killing-teen-daughter-in-murder-suicide/
201. "Ava Wood ran fast, shared her gummies, and made friends laugh." Syracuse.com. January 21, 2023.
https://www.syracuse.com/crime/2023/01/ava-wood-ran-fast-shared-her-gummies-and-made-friends-laugh-trying-hard-was-her-thing.html
202. Rashad Lavan Carr obituary.
https://www.hamiltonsfuneralhome.com/services/services_detail.aspx?rid=63401
203. McFettridge, Scott, and Hollingworth, Heather. "Police" Shooting that killed 2 at youth program was targeted." Associated Press. January 24, 2023.
https://apnews.com/article/law-enforcement-crime-des-moines-shootings-teens-7a4243dffc9103fdb11dbf94f0702ed7
204. "Teenager dead after shooting at 9th and Atkinson." WISN.com. January 23, 2023.
https://www.wisn.com/article/15-year-old-milwaukee-teen-shot-and-killed/42617629
205. "Mother of 15-year-old boy killed in Milwaukee wants gun violence to stop." WISNNews.com.
https://www.youtube.com/watch?v=_3QXOlw3h5M
206. Freeman, Laila. "Two charged in Santa Fe County murder." KRQE.com. January 26, 2023.
https://www.krqe.com/news/crime/two-charged-in-santa-fe-county-murder/
207. Lederman, Nathan. "Sheriff's office arrests 2 men in teen's slaying at Camel Tracks." Santa Fe New Mexican. January 26, 2023.

https://www.santafenewmexican.com/news/local_news/sheriffs-office-arrests-two-men-in-teens-slaying-at-camel-tracks/article_ce78916e-9d9a-11ed-9876-7b979dacceae.html
208. Hayes, John. "Broken Arrow Police, Tulsa District Attorney share input on youth violence." KTUL.com. February 8, 2023.
https://ktul.com/news/local/broken-arrow-police-tulsa-district-attorney-share-input-on-youth-violence
209. Childress, Autumn. "Police say murder of Midlothian teen was not random, family speaks out." WRIC. January 31, 2023.
https://www.wric.com/news/local-news/chesterfield-coubunty/police-say-murder-of-midlothian-teen-was-not-random-family-speaks-out/
210. Green, Kendall. "Family of teen slain outraged after delayed notice from police, school district." WMAR2News.com. January 23, 2023.
https://www.wmar2news.com/local/family-of-teen-slain-outraged-after-delayed-notice-from-police-school-district
211. "Family of teenager killed in a shooting near Forest Park High School speaks out." WBAL.com. January 27, 2023.
https://www.wbal.com/article/601627/124/family-of-a-teenager-killed-in-a-shooting-near-forest-park-high-school-speaks-out
212. May, Maya. "Family of 15-year-old shooting victim mourn teen with a bright future." WTOL11.com. February 6, 2023.
https://www.wtol.com/article/news/local/donald-hogan-family-remembers-15-year-old-toledo-shooting-victim/512-f7a39393-4912-47cf-8098-d433dafed1c6
213.Coroner's report. Lucas County Ohio. Anthony Krug-Overton. January 26, 2023.
https://www.co.lucas.oh.us/CivicAlerts.aspx?AID=1743
214. Van Gilder, Rachel. "News Report on teens Grand Rapids death led mom to call police." Woodtv.com. January 26, 2023.
https://www.woodtv.com/news/kent-county/teen-found-shot-dead-in-east-grand-rapids-street-idd/
215.Marigny, Dianté." Cameron County DA: death of Santa Rosa County teen linked to 'criminal enterprise.'" KRGV.com. February 17, 2023.
https://www.krgv.com/news/cameron-county-da-death-of-santa-rosa-teen-linked-to-criminal-enterprise-/
216. Couvillion, Ellyn. "13-year-old dies from wounds from shooting on Thursday, East Baton Rouge officials say." The Advocate. January 31, 2023.
https://www.theadvocate.com/baton_rouge/news/juvenile-shooting-victim-dies-of-injury-ebr-officials-say/article_e7ff7e96-a17c-11ed-a142-5bdf8d393b28.html
217. "Neighbors rush to help after teen shot, killed in Kannapolis; 14-year-old arrested." WSOCTV.com. February 2, 2023.
https://www.wsoctv.com/news/local/17-year-old-killed-2-juveniles-hurt-kannapolis-shooting-police-say/2lBGEVUY4BBCFPSVRGMDWJPSA4/
218. Honeycutt, Jordan. "3 charged in connection to January shooting deaths of 2 teens in Albuquerque." KRQE.com. April 5, 2023.
https://www.krqe.com/news/crime/3-charged-in-connection-to-january-shooting-deaths-of-two-teens-in-albuquerque/
219. "Arlington teen arrested after another teen shot to death in Alexandria." ARLnow.com. January 30, 2023.
https://www.arlnow.com/2023/01/30/arlington-teen-arrested-after-another-teen-shot-to-death-in-alexandria/
220. "Notes: teen shot and killed in West End hotel." ALXnow.com. January 30, 2023.
https://www.alxnow.com/2023/01/30/notes-teen-shot-and-killed-in-west-end-hotel/
221. Lepp, Mike and Adams, Richard. "13-year-old Jefferson County shooting victim A'Rhianna Moye dies." WJBF.com. January 30, 2023.
https://www.wjbf.com/news/crime-news/13-year-old-jefferson-county-shooting-victim-arhianna-moye-dies/
222. "13-year-old Georgia girl dies after police say she was shot by her own brother." WSBTV.com. January 31, 2023. https://sports.yahoo.com/13-old-georgia-girl-dies-183218669.html
223. "Police investigate fatal shooting of teen." Southwest Messenger Press. February 8, 2023.
https://www.southwestmessengerpress.com/articles/news/police-investigate-fatal-shooting-of-teen/

224. Bixler, Lance. "Boy and man killed in Pomona shooting ID'd." Vigour Times. January 30, 2023. https://vigourtimes.com/boy-and-man-killed-in-pomona-shooting-idd/
225. Rojas, Javier. "God's Pantry becomes a lifeline for needy families during pandemic." Daily Bulletin. December 18, 2020.
https://www.dailybulletin.com/2020/12/18/gods-pantry-becomes-lifeline-for-needy-pomona-families-durin g-pandemic/
226. "Teen dead in shooting along Tucson bike path." KVOA.com. January 30, 2023.
https://www.kvoa.com/news/teen-dead-in-shooting-along-tucson-bike-path/article_76a764ee-a0f9-11ed-a97a-e727c3d34855.html#:~:text=TUCSON%20(KVOA)%20%2D%0A%2015,Road%20and%20North %201st%20Avenue.
227. Donnelly, Jamie. "Two boys linked to Tucson killing." Tucson.com. March 29, 2023.
https://tucson.com/news/local/crime-and-courts/two-boys-linked-to-tucson-killing/article_6ad21c02-ce73-11ed-9150-231af3538bc0.html
228. Basco, Isabella. "'He was perfect'|Family of teen killed in Austin hookah lounge shooting speaks out." KVUE.com. March 14, 2023.
https://www.kvue.com/article/news/community/brayden-bolyard-family-hookah-lounge-shooting/269-186 52127-2286-48f5-910a-e465618179bf
229. Jones, Abigail and Russ, Juliana. "Suspect in northwest Austin hookah lounge shooting arrested, charged with capital murder." KXAN.com. March 13, 2023.
https://www.kxan.com/news/crime/police-arrest-suspect-in-northwest-austin-hookah-lounge-shooting/
230. Brayden Robert Bolyard obituary.
https://www.dignitymemorial.com/obituaries/georgetown-tx/brayden-bolyard-11135195
231. Osborn, Claire. "19-year-old charged in shooting deaths of 2 Jarrell High students at Austin hookah lounge," Austin-American Statesman. March 21, 2023.
https://www.statesman.com/story/news/local/2023/03/13/christian-stevens-charged-fatal-shooting-jarrell-high-football-players-hookah-lounge-austin/70004922007/
232. Ferrando, Erika. "'They took my best friend'- teen remembers 15-year-old lost to weekend gunshot." WWLTV.com. January 30, 2023.
https://www.wwltv.com/article/news/crime/new-orleans-kennedi-belton-killed-crime-warren-easton/289-c9 134ef6-ad48-4157-9022-3b72ae250e0b
233. "Pennsylvania teen once hailed as hero killed by accidental gunshot, police say: 'a tragic, tragic situation.'" CBSNews.com. February 1, 2023.
https://www.cbsnews.com/news/anthony-alexander-jr-pennsylvania-teen-hero-killed-accidental-gunshot/
224.Bjorkgren, David. "Teen Anthony Alexander up for young hero award remembered."
Delco.today.com. February 2, 2023. https://delco.today/2023/02/anthony-alexander-young-hero/
225. Rieck, Dana. "Teen killed in triple shooting at East St. Louis church." St. Louis Post-Dispatch. January 30, 2023.
https://www.stltoday.com/news/local/crime-and-courts/teen-killed-in-triple-shooting-at-east-st-louis-churc h/article_599b3ac9-3e9e-53d6-a7dd-c1d0060ea11f.html#:~:text=Devon%20Montgomery%2C%2016%2 C%20was%20also,were%20also%20shot%20but%20survived.
226. Aayad, Osama and Barczewski, Laura. "16-year-old killed in shooting in East St. Louis church." KDSK.com. January 30, 2023.
https://www.ksdk.com/article/news/crime/1-dead-2-wounded-during-sunday-church-service-shooting-in-e sl/63-6a0899c0-08a8-4dfb-a388-8b7f283be3c6
227. Axelrod, Ben and Buckley, Bri. "13-year-old fatally shot, 15-year-old shot and injured in Bedford." WKYC.com. January 30, 2023.
https://www.wkyc.com/article/news/crime/13-year-old-fatally-shot-15-year-old-shot-injured-bedford/95-09 126bb7-b7da-48d2-b2e1-c1ac99488e1b
228. Hysheen Thomas, Jr., GoFundMe.
229. Saltonstall, Gus. "17-year-old shot and killed in Harlem: Police." Patch. January 30, 2023.
https://patch.com/new-york/harlem/17-year-old-shot-killed-harlem-police
230. "Csean Skerritt fired 5 shots in murder of 13-year-old Tyler Lawrencein Mattapan prosecutor says." CBSnews.com. February 17, 2023.
https://www.cbsnews.com/boston/news/csean-skerritt-arraignment-murder-13-year-old-tyler-lawrence-m attapan-norwood-massachusetts/

231. "'My heart is hurting': Birmingham High School senior mourned following deadly weekend shooting, suspect charged." AL.com. February 1, 2023.
https://www.al.com/news/birmingham/2023/01/my-heart-is-hurting-birmingham-high-school-senior-mourned-following-deadly-weekend-shooting-suspect-charged.html
232. Hermann, Peter. "Two children were accidentally shot in D.C. Police haven't found either gun." The Washington Post. January 30, 2023.
https://www.washingtonpost.com/dc-md-va/2023/01/30/dc-children-shot-guns/
233. Coleman, Chris. "Update: 2 17-year-olds shot in Bridgeton, NJ; Man killed, woman wounded." WPGtalkradio.com. January 29, 023.
https://wpgtalkradio.com/two-17-year-olds-shot-in-bridgeton-nj-man-killed-woman-wounded/
234. McCoy, Malaysia, and Raines, Brandon. "Vicksburg issues curfew after 13-year-old killed in shooting." WJTV.com. January 31, 2023.
https://www.wjtv.com/news/local-news/vicksburg-issues-curfew-after-13-year-old-killed-in-shooting/
235. "2 killed including teen in Elkhart shooting." WNDU.com. January 30, 2023.
https://www.wndu.com/2023/01/30/elkhart-county-homicide-unit-investigating-fatal-shooting/
236. "Identity of 13-year-old shot and killed in Decatur released." Newschannel20.com. February 1, 2023.
https://newschannel20.com/news/local/identity-of-13-year-old-shot-and-killed-in-decatur-released-marquez-n-otis
237. Reid, Tony." Decatur child shot dead by brother playing around with gun, inquest hears." Hearald & Review. March 8, 2023.
https://herald-review.com/news/local/crime-and-courts/decatur-child-shot-dead-by-brother-playing-around-with-gun-inquest-hears/article_a2e7f482-bde7-11ed-9cbd-0bfb596839cf.html
238. Marquez N, Otis obituary.
https://www.legacy.com/us/obituaries/name/marquez-otis-obituary?id=39852298.
238. Family of Montevius Goss wants people to know who he was." February 2, 2023.
https://www.youtube.com/watch?v=nWo7th_dvuo
239.Ball, Biannca. "Body found in Louisville identified as 16-year-old." WJTV.com. February 2, 2023.
https://www.wjtv.com/news/state/body-found-in-louisville-identified-as-missing-16-year-old/
240. Amhara, Chernéy. "2 Dead, including teen after car riddled with bullets in Golden Glades shooting." NBCMiami.com. February 1, 2023.
https://www.nbcmiami.com/news/local/2-dead-including-teen-after-car-riddled-with-bullets-in-golden-glades-shooting/2963008/
241. "Hutto Police provide update on fatal Lakeside Estates shooting." City of Hutto. February 15, 2023.
https://www.huttotx.gov/CivicAlerts.aspx?AID=152
242. "Firearms are the Number One Cause of Death for Children in the United States but Rank No Higher than FIfth in Other Industrialized Nations." Kaiser Family Foundation. July 8, 2022.
https://www.kff.org/health-reform/press-release/firearms-are-the-leading-cause-of-death-for-children-in-the-united-states-but-rank-no-higher-than-fifth-in-other-industrialized-nations/

About the Author

Carol Bengle Gilbert is an author and attorney. This was not supposed to be Carol's next book. There's "an airplane read" in the hopper. But her anguish on hearing about one kid after another shot to death caused her to change course.

What other country sees 150 of its children die from bullets in a single month? None. In Ukraine, which is actively fighting a war on its soil, 8 children died in the period January 1-January 29, 2023, the same number that died in America on January 1 alone. Nowhere else in the world do adults shrug off kids being shot to death every day. Nowhere else in the world excluding perhaps active armed conflict zones do the adults assume they are powerless to keep children safe. Nowhere else in the world do the adults make excuses instead of ensuring children's wellbeing.

We are smart and compassionate people. It's too late for the children of January but we can still save June's children, July's children, all the children who will suffer needless pain and death from bullets, by making children's lives our priority. If we start today, we can save 1,050 children by year's end.

By writing this book, and jumping it up in the queue, Carol hopes to focus our hearts and minds on valuing each one of our country's children and rescuing those who would otherwise be sacrificed to bullets.

Carol is the author of *En Route to Knockaderry*, a spirited search for ancestors and a most unusual genealogical memoir.

www.carolbenglegilbert.com
authorcarolbenglegilbert@gmail.com